MW00940648

Cooking After Weight Loss Surgery

Amy Solen

Copyright © 2014 Amy Solen

All rights reserved.

ISBN: 1494290987

ISBN-13: 978-1494290986

DEDICATION

This book is dedicated first to and foremost to God. Thank you for giving me life and the opportunity to experience it to the fullest. I love you and thank you for sending me your only Son, Jesus to save me. Next it is dedicated to my wonderful husband and children. They were great sports when I would try many new recipes and they were the guinea pigs for trying the good and bad ones. And finally I wish to dedicate this to my physicians who were able to take care of me and perform the surgery that essentially saved my life. Thank you!

CONTENTS

ACKNOWLEDGMENTS

I would like to thank all the recipe contributors, whether they chose to be named or not, I do appreciate your contribution to this collection of recipes. I also want to thank the dieticians who help WLS patients everyday with our journeys to a healthy lifestyle. You can't even begin to imagine how much we appreciate you and your work.

1 HOW TO USE THIS BOOK

While the main focus of this book is to be a recipe book for people who have had weight loss surgery or who are about to have weight loss surgery there are a few things you should know before using this book. First, all temperatures listed in this book are in Fahrenheit. Second, substitutions can be made for common ingredients, such as sugar, see page 4 for such substitution suggestions.

This book calls for users to have certain kitchen gadgets or utensils that will make your journey easier, in the long run. Here is a brief list of what helped (and continues to help) me on my way:
1. Immersion blender
2. Regular blender
3. Food Processor
4. Dutch Oven
5. Canning materials (mason jars, lids and caps, large pot)
6. Slow cooker (at least a 4 quart)

These items can be found at your local discount store such as Kmart or Wal-Mart, if you don't already have them. The most important item on this list would most definitely be the immersion blender for the mushy phase of the WLS diet. That gadget alone saved me!

Before starting this or any diet, be sure to check with your physician to make sure it is ok and in your best interest to begin a plan such as this. This book is not meant to substitute any information provided by a doctor but to be a recipe book only from someone who has went through weight loss surgery herself.

Recipe Substitutions:

Recipe calls for:	Substitution:
1 c. mayonnaise	½ c. mayonnaise + ½ c. low-fat or fat-free yogurt
1 c. margarine or butter	½ c. margarine or butter + ¼ c. water
1 c. sour cream	½ c. sour cream + ½ c. low-fat or fat-free yogurt
2 large eggs	3 egg whites
Whole milk	Fat-free milk or lactose free milk or soy milk, etc.
Sugar	Sugar substitute such as Splenda® or Truvia® if desired

Did you know?
Proteins have about 4 calories per gram. (115 calories per ounce)
Carbs have about 4 calories per gram. (115 calories per ounce)
Fats have about 9 calorie per gram. (225 calories per ounce)

Measurement guide:

Cup =	Fluid oz =	Tbsp =	tsp =	Milliliter =
1 c.	8 oz	16 T	48 tsp	237 ml
¾ c	6 oz	12 T	36 tsp	177 ml
2/3 c	5 1/3 oz	10.6 T	32 tsp	158 ml
½ c	4 oz	8 T	24 tsp	118 ml
1/3 c	2 2/3 oz	5.3 T	16 tsp	79 ml
¼ c	2 oz	4 T	12 tsp	59 ml
1/8 c	1 oz	2 T	6 tsp	30 ml
1/16 c	½ oz	1 T	3 tsp	15 ml

Common abbreviations used in this book:

Teaspoon	tsp
Tablespoon	T
Cup	c
Large	lrg or lg
Packet	pkt
Package	pkg
Ounce	oz
Quart	qt

2 APPETIZERS AND BEVERAGES

Liquid Phase

CHOCOLATE COFFEE
2 T. instant coffee
3 c. milk
1/4 c. sugar or artificial sweetener
1 c. water
1 scoop unflavored protein
dash of salt (optional)
2 (1oz) sq. unsweetened chocolate
In a saucepan, combine coffee, sugar, salt, chocolate, protein and water. Stir over low heat until chocolate has melted. Simmer 4 minutes, stirring constantly. Gradually add milk, stirring until heated. When hot, remove from heat and beat with rotary beater until frothy. Pour into cups and top with whipped cream, that may be stirred until melted. Yield: 3 servings.

CHOCOLATE SHAKE
1 tsp. chocolate flavoring
1 scoop ice cream (optional)
1 tsp. sweetener
1 scoop protein (chocolate or any flavor)
6 oz. milk
Combine all ingredients in blender, blend until smooth.

DENISE'S SUGARFREE EGGNOG

Denise at muschealth.com
4 c. skim milk (or fat free lactose-free milk)
6 pkts Splenda
2 tsp. vanilla extract
1 c. fat free egg substitute (like EggBeaters)
1/2 tsp. ground nutmeg
3 1. vanilla sugar free, fat free instant pudding
Place all ingredients in the blender and blend for 30-60 seconds or until smooth. Chill for several hours. Shake or stir eggnog well to blend. Serve in glasses or mugs.
Note: Yield: 5- 1 cup (8 oz) servings Calories: 97 Fat: 0 g Protein: 11 g Carbs: 11g

HIGH PROTEIN HOT CHOCOLATE

1 pkt hot chocolate powder
1 c. boiling water
100% whey protein powder mini marshmallows (optional)
Put the hot chocolate packet in a mug. Add about 1/2 scoop (1T of protein powder) to mug. Add the 1 cup of boiling water. Add marshmallows. Stir until no chunks

KYLIE'S EGGNOG

Kylie at muschealth.com
5 c. light vanilla soymilk
6 pkts Splenda®
1 pkg (1 oz.) vanilla sugar free, fat free instant pudding
1 tsp. rum extract
1/2 tsp. ground nutmeg
In a blender, combine all ingredients and blend on high until mixed thoroughly. Refrigerate for a few hours to allow to thicken.
Note: Yield: 5- 1 cup (8 oz) servings Calories: 88 Fat: 1 g Protein: 6 g Carbs: 6.5 g

MINTY SUMMER SMOOTHIE
muschealth.com
1/2 c. ripe honeydew melon (diced)
6 fresh mint leaves
1/2 c. plain, fat-free yogurt
1/4 c. cucumber (peeled, seeded and diced)
1 pkt. artificial sweetener
2 ice cubes
Put all ingredients in a blender and purée until smooth. Add ice cubes and blend on high speed for about 30 seconds until chilled. Garnish with mint leaf if desired.
Note: Yields: 1 serving Calories: 140 Fat: 0.5 g Protein: 10 g

SHARON'S MANGO-GINGER SMOOTHIE
Sharon at muschealth.com
2 ripe mangoes (about 3/4 lb each) or 1 mango and 1 banana
1 cup low-fat buttermilk
1 (8oz) container low-fat, light vanilla yogurt
2 pieces crystallized ginger, about 1 oz
handful of chipped ice
Cut mango into pieces, stand it on end and slice the flesh off both sides of the central pit. Lay each half on a cutting board and with the tip of your knife, score the flesh in a cross-hatch pattern. Pushing from the skin side, turn inside out so that the mango flesh pops up; slice it off the skin. Also cut off the remaining flesh from around the pit and remove the skin. In a blender, purée the fruit and ginger, scraping down the sides as necessary. Add the buttermilk, yogurt and ice and purée until smooth and frothy.
Note: Yields: 4 servings Calories: 120 Fat: 1 g Protein: 4 g Carb: 25 g (2 g fiber)

STRAWBERRY LEMONADE
One tub Crystal Light® Lemonade sugar-free drink mix
6-8 frozen strawberries
Add two quarts of water to the Crystal Light drink mix in a decorative pitcher. Add frozen strawberries and allow flavors and color to develop while chilling in the refrigerator for at least two hours or preferably overnight.

TIRAMISU COFFEE

4 oz. semisweet chocolate chips
1/2 c. powdered sugar
16 oz freshly brewed coffee or espresso
1 tsp. almond extract
4 to 5 oz coffee liqueur
8 oz heavy whipping cream
1 T. grated chocolate

Melt chocolate chips in double boiler with 1/2 cup coffee. Remove from heat and let stand until fully melted and creamy. Meanwhile, mix together cream, sugar and almond extract in a medium bowl, beat at medium-high speed until soft peaks form. Divide chocolate mixture into 4 coffee cups. Stir in remaining coffee. Add liqueur and top with whipped cream. Garnish with grated chocolate.

VANILLA SHAKE

1 tsp. vanilla extract
6 oz. milk
1 scoop protein (any flavor or flavorless)
1 scoop vanilla ice cream (optional) or 6 ice cubes
1 tsp. sweetener

Combine all ingredients in blender and blend until smooth.

WATERMELON SANGRIA

3 lbs seedless watermelon, peeled and cubed, plus 1/2 lb watermelon cut into wedges
6 oz vodka
Lime simple syrup (see below)
Ice
1 bottle dry white wine

Lime simple syrup - made by heating 1/2 cup Truvia® with juice of 3 limes and 1/2 cup water, straining and cooling. In a blender, purée the watermelon cubes. Pour through a fine strainer into a pitcher. Add the white wine, vodka, and lime syrup. Stir and refrigerate for at least 2 hours. Stir again, then pour the sangria into ice-filled white wine glasses and garnish with watermelon wedges.

Mushy Phase

CON QUESO DIP
1 lb Velveeta® cheese
2 whole jalapeño peppers, slit open and seeded
1/2 c. hot picante sauce
1/4 tsp Tabasco® or other hot sauce
Put the cheese in a 1-quart microwave-safe dish and microwave at full power to melt, about 5 minutes, stirring midway through. Stir in the picante sauce and hot sauce. garnish with jalapeño peppers.

CRAB RANGOON CUPS
12 fresh wonton wrappers
1 T. chopped roasted red pepper (optional)
2 tsp. peanut oil
6 oz. fresh picked crab
1/2 tsp Sriracha sauce plus additional to taste (optional)
4 oz reduced fat cream cheese, softened
Sea salt and freshly ground black pepper to taste
4 scallions, minced (optional)
Lightly brush wontons with peanut oil and fit into your mini muffin cups. Bake in preheated 375° oven for five minutes, until beginning to brown on edges. Remove from oven to cool while preparing filling. Blend crab, cream cheese, scallions, roasted red pepper and Sriracha - season lightly with salt and pepper, adding additional Sriracha to taste. Divide crab into cups. Bake an additional 8 to 10 minutes, until wonton is golden and filling is melted.

CURRY VEGETABLE DIP
1 c. reduced fat sour cream
2 T. prepared yellow mustard
1/2 c. mayonnaise
1 tsp. curry powder
1 T. fresh lemon juice
1/2 tsp. paprika
2 T. chopped parsley
1/2 tsp. tarragon
2 T. grated white onion
salt and pepper to taste
1 T. minced chives

In a bowl, blend the sour cream, mayonnaise, and lemon juice. Mix in the parsley, onion, chives, mustard, curry powder, paprika, tarragon, salt and pepper. Add hot sauce to taste, cover and chill for at least 1 hour in the refrigerator or 15 minutes in the freezer.

DOUG'S EDAMAME HUMMUS
Doug at muschealth.com
1 (12oz) pkg fresh or frozen, shelled edamame
1/2 tsp. cumin
1 T. fresh cilantro (or 1/2 tsp. dried cilantro)
3-4 large garlic cloves
1/4 c. water
1/8 tsp. red pepper flakes
1/4 c. tahini (sesame seed paste)
2 T. chopped fresh flat leaf parsley (divided)
zest from 1 lemon
juice from 1 lemon
3 T. olive oil
3/4 tsp. kosher salt

Boil the soybeans and whole garlic cloves in salted water for 4 minutes. Drain and rinse with cold water. In a food processor (or blender), purée the edamame, garlic, water, tahini, lemon zest, lemon juice, salt, cumin, cilantro, pepper flakes, and 1 Tbsp. of parsley until smooth. With motor running, slowly add in olive oil until combined. Transfer to a serving dish and stir in the remaining 1 Tbsp. of parsley.
Note: Yields: 10 (1/4 cup) servings Calories: 110 Fat: 9 g Protein: 5 g Carb: 4 g (2 g fiber)

HUMMUS

**1 - 16 oz can chickpeas or garbanzo beans, very well
drained**
sesame paste
2 garlic cloves, crushed
1/2 tsp. salt
Juice of two lemons, about 4 T.
2 T. olive oil
4 T. tahini

Combine the chickpeas, lemon juice, tahini, garlic, and salt in blender
or food processor. Slowly add olive oil then 1/4 cup of water, blending
for 3 to 5 minutes on low until creamy and smooth. Adding a bit more
water if needed. Transfer to a serving bowl, and create a shallow well
in the center of the hummus. Drizzle with the remaining 1 tablespoon
of olive oil. Garnish with parsley. Serve immediately with fresh
cucumber
`chips', or mini peppers, warm or toasted pita bread, or cover and
refrigerate for later. For a spicier hummus, add a dash of cayenne
pepper.

JENN'S ITALIAN CHEESE

Jenn at muschealth.com
1/4 c. fat-free cottage cheese
1/4 c. shredded mozzarella
3 T. marinara sauce cheese (low-fat/part skim)
3 T. frozen chopped spinach, thawed

Mix ingredients and microwave until cheese is melted. It tastes just
like lasagna!
Note: Yields: 1 serving Calories: 160 Fat: 6 g Protein: 17 g Carb: 9 g
(2 g fiber)

Solid Phase

BACON WRAPPED JALAPEÑO POPPERS
12 large jalapeño peppers
3 green onions, very finely minced
4 ounces reduced fat cream cheese, room temperature
12 slices bacon
1/2 cup shredded sharp cheddar cheese - reduced fat
Cut each pepper in half lengthwise - scoop out seeds and membranes with a spoon. Blend cream cheese, cheddar, and green onion until smooth - chill mixture to firm. Spoon out a small portion of cheese filling, rolling the into a small pepper shaped bullet, filling one half of the
pepper and topping with the other half to enclose cheese filling. Do not overfill. Wrap a slice of bacon around the pepper, overlapping slightly. Secure ends with a small bamboo skewer or toothpick and arrange on baking sheet that has been sprayed with nonstick spray. Can be refrigerated at this point until ready to cook. Preheat oven to 400 degrees and roast the peppers 25 to 30 minutes, until bacon is browned and jalapeños are softened. Serve hot.

BAKED TOMATOES
5-6 large tomatoes
Greek seasoning
Olive oil spray
1/4 c. pine nuts (optional)
1/4 c. low fat parmesan cheese
Preheat oven to 350°. Cut tomatoes in half-lengthwise and place open face in non-stick 9x13 pan. Spray surface of tomatoes with olive oil spray. Coat with cheese and pine nuts. Sprinkle on Greek seasoning to taste. Bake for 50 minutes on middle rack.
Note: Calories: 73 Total Fat: 5 g Total Carbohydrates: 6 g Dietary Fiber: 2 g Sugars: 0 g Protein: 3 g

BLT ROMA BOATS

10 Roma tomatoes, split lengthwise
3/4 c. low-fat mayonnaise or Miracle Whip® salad dressing
1/2 lb strip bacon, fried crisp
4 c. iceberg lettuce, finely shredded

Spoon out seeds and membrane of the Roma halves. Finely chop bacon in food processor. Shred lettuce with a hand grater or use grating blade in a food processor. In large mixing bowl, combine lettuce, bacon and mayonnaise. If it's too dry, add a little buttermilk or more mayonnaise. Spoon into Roma halves and put on a platter. Garnish with paprika or parsley if desired.
Note: Makes 10 appetizer servings.

CRAB WONTONS

4 oz reduced-fat cream cheese, softened
3 tablespoons soy sauce
1/4 teaspoon sesame oil
3 green onions, thinly sliced
1 teaspoon sugar or Splenda®
1 cup crab meat or 1 cup cooked chopped shrimp
1 teaspoon dried crushed red pepper
1 tablespoon Asian hot sauce (Sriracha)
1 teaspoon green onion, finely chopped
1 package won ton wrappers

Preheat oven to 400. Mix cream cheese, green onion, crab and hot sauce in a small bowl. Put about 1 1/2 teaspoon of mixture in center of each wrapper. Dip finger tips in water and wet edges of wrapper lightly and fold in half - try to remove as much air as possible. Seal tightly and place won tons on baking sheet coated with cooking spray. Bake until they start to brown - should be about 15 to 20 minutes. While they cook, make the dipping sauce.

DEVILED EGGS

6 hard-boiled eggs
1/4 tsp. salt
2 T. mayonnaise
1/4 tsp. paprika, or sprinkled on
1 tsp. vinegar each for look
1/2 tsp. dry mustard
1/8 tsp. pepper

Cut the eggs in half lengthwise. Remove the yolks, reserving the egg whites. Put the yolks in a bowl and mix with mayonnaise, vinegar, mustard, salt, paprika, and pepper. Mashing the yolks in the process. Divide the mixture among the cavities of the whites. Cover and refrigerate until well chilled. Makes 12 deviled eggs.

HOT CHILI SALSA

5 lbs tomatoes, peeled and diced
1 lb onions, diced
1 c. vinegar
2 lbs peppers, assorted (hot and non-hot), diced
3 tsp. salt
1/2 tsp. pepper

Put all ingredients into a large saucepan. Heat to a boil and simmer 10 minutes. Fill hot jars, leaving 1/2 - inch head space. Remove air bubbles. Wipe jar rim. Store in refrigerator or can for extended storage.

Note: Yield: 6-8 pints

PARMESAN CRISPS

1 c. freshly grated Parmesan pepper to taste (optional)

You can use a sheet pan lined with parchment paper or a mini muffin tin to make perfect crisps. Preheat the oven to 300 degrees. Place a tablespoon of cheese into the bottom of each muffin spot and press down to compress slightly with a shot glass or spice jar. Sprinkle pepper on top. Bake 6 to 8 minutes, until golden.

STUFFED MUSHROOMS

bariatriceating.com

I T. olive oil
I sm. onion, finely chopped - or two shallots
12 large `stuffing' mushroom caps, stems removed, chopped and reserved
1/4 c. chopped red pepper
1/4 c. chopped flat leaf parsley
salt and pepper
1/4 c. Italian flavored panko bread crumbs
6 oz. Italian sausage - about 2/3 pkg
1/4 c. grated Parmesan cheese or Romano cheese
3 garlic cloves, chopped

In a large nonstick skillet, heat I tablespoon olive oil. Sauté mushroom caps smooth side down over medium high heat for 3 to 4 minutes or until tops are lightly browned and liquid stats to accumulate in cap. Carefully turn the brown edges of cup side, I to 2 minutes - liquid will evaporate. Place cooked mushroom cup side down on paper towels to drain. Brown sausage in same skillet, mashing with fork while cooking so that the mixture has a fine texture. Pour off any accumulated fat.

Add chopped mushroom stems, garlic, onion, and red pepper; continue cooking over medium high heat until vegetables are softened and juices have evaporated, about 10 minutes. Remove from heat, and when mixture has cooled enough to handle, toss with parsley, bread crumbs and cheese until well combined; season with salt and pepper. Arrange caps cup side up in a large baking dish and lightly season with salt and pepper. Pack with sausage mixture. Dish may be prepared in advance, covered and chilled until ready to bake. When ready to serve, preheat oven to 400°. Cover dish with foil and bake 10 to 12 minutes to heat mushrooms through.

Note: Purée in a blender to enjoy during mushy phase.

SUMMER SALSA

1 clove garlic
1 jalapeño pepper, stemmed and minced
2 tsp. salt, divided
4 medium ripe tomatoes, cored and diced
1/4 c. chopped fresh cilantro
White corn tortilla chips, for dipping
1/4 medium red onion, finely diced

Smash the garlic clove, sprinkle with 1 tsp. salt, and, with flat side of knife, mash and smear the mixture to a coarse paste. Combine the garlic mixture, tomatoes, onion, jalapeño, and cilantro in a serving bowl.

Season with the remaining 1 tsp. salt, adding more to taste, if necessary. Serve immediately with tortilla chips (or use as a burger topping), or to allow the flavors to blend, cover and set aside for one hour at room temperature.

3 SOUPS AND SALADS

Liquid Phase

CHICKEN & RICE WITH WHITE BEANS SOUP

2 skinless, boneless chicken breasts (16 oz total), cut into bite size pieces
1/4 c. brown rice (uncooked)
1/4 c. wild rice (uncooked)
1/4 c. farro (uncooked)
2 carrots cleaned and sliced
1/4 c. quinoa (uncooked)
7 stalks of celery, sliced
2 tsp Bragg Liquid Amino (or to taste)
1 large onion, diced (optional)
1/4 c. dry navy beans
Sea salt, pepper and parsley to taste
1/4 c. dry garbanzo (chick peas)
1/4 c. dry pearl barley
water

Add 2 cups of water to a 5 quart soup pot. Add all other ingredients & turn burner to high to start boiling. Add more water to fill pot to within 1 - 11/2 inches from top. Bring to rolling boil. Put lid on & turn burner down to a strong simmer. Remove lid & stir occasionally. If the water boils down, add more water to bring the level back up.
Continue cooking until all beans and grains are done. This should be about 3 hours. I let it simmer on low heat & stir occasionally so it won't stick. Serving Size:

makes 12 12-oz servings.
Note: Strain for liquid phase, blend for purée or mushy phase.
CALORIES: 105.1 | FAT: 0.7 g | PROTEIN: 80.2 g | CARBS: 31.7 g |
FIBER: 3.2 g

CHICKEN STOCK
1 chicken carcass
2 parsnips, chunked (optional)
2 carrots, cut into chunks
1 head garlic
2 stalks celery, chunked
2 chicken wings
2 onions, chunked
water, as needed
Place the carcass, carrots, celery, onions, parsnips, garlic, and wings
into a 6 quart slow cooker. Fill with water until it is 2" below the top.
Cover and cook on low for 10 hours. Strain into a large container.
Discard the solids. Refrigerate the stock overnight. The next day
scoop off any fat that has floated to the top. Discard the fat. Freeze or
refrigerate the broth until ready to use.
   Note: Per 1 cup: Calories: 60; Fat: 1.5g; Carbs: 10g; Protein: 3g

CHOW DOWN CHOWDER
1 (20oz) pkg. refrigerated shredded potatoes
1/3c. sliced green onions
1/4 tsp. pepper
1 (14.5oz) can reduced-sodium chicken broth
12oz. 97% fat free cooked link sausage, halved lengthwise
1 (10oz) pkg frozen whole kernel and sliced (optional)
corn hot sauce to taste (optional)
2 c. skim milk
In a 4qt Dutch oven, combine potatoes, broth and corn. Bring mixture
to a boil; reduce heat. Simmer, covered, for 10 minutes or until
potatoes are just tender, stirring occasionally. Using a potato masher,
slightly mash potatoes. Stir in remaining ingredients. Strain for liquid
phase or use a potato masher to bring consistency to mushy. Enjoy.

CLAM CHOWDER

2 cans minced clams
3 cans cream of potato soup
2 stalks celery, ends cut off
I sm. carton whipping cream
I medium onion
2 c. milk
4 medium red potatoes, diced
salt and pepper to taste
Sauté onion and celery in margarine. Cook potatoes until done,slightly mushy. Add onion and celery to potato water. Add remaining ingredients. Cook for 20 minutes or until potatoes are mushy. Use an immersion blender to purée soup. Add water if necessary.

FISH STOCK

3 quarts of water
2 stalks celery, chopped
3 fish heads and bones, any type
2 T. ground black pepper
I bunch of parsley or I T. dried parsley
2 onions, peeled and quartered
Put all ingredients into a large cooking pot and heat to boiling. Reduce heat to low and simmer for 5-6 hours. Remove all solids and refrigerate overnight. Skim off any foam that appeared overnight. Refrigerate, use or freeze.
Note: Can be used in replacement of any recipe calling for chicken stock. Calories: 430; Fat: 10g; Carbs: 37g; Protein: 52g; Fiber: 7g.

FRENCH ONION SOUP

Wende Sumner
4 large onions, peeled and 3 T. flour
sliced thin 2 quarts beef stock or chicken
I/2 T. butter or margarine stock
I/2 T. olive oil
Place onions, butter, oil, and flour into a medium size cooking pot. Cook until well blended. Add stock and cook on medium to medium-low heat for 40 minutes. Strain mixture and enjoy.

GUMBO

2 T. butter
2 T. Cajun seasoning
2 T. flour
4 chicken andouille sausages, sliced
1 cubanelle pepper, diced
(optional)
1 1/2 c. diced fresh tomatoes
4 cloves garlic, diced
2 c. diced okra
1 onion, diced
4 carrots, peeled and diced
2 stalks celery, diced
1 qt. chicken stock (see chicken
stock recipe)

In a nonstick skillet, melt the butter. Add the flour and stir until the flour is golden brown. Add the pepper, garlic, onions, carrots, and celery. Sauté for 1 minutes. Add the mixture to a 4-quart slow cooker. Add the stock, seasoning, sausage, and tomatoes. Cook on low for 8-10 hours. Add the okra for the last hour of cooking. Stir prior to serving. Strain for liquid phase, use immersion blender for mushy phase, serve as is for solid phase.

Note: Calories: 130; Fat: 6g; Carbs: 14g; Protein: 6g;

HOMEMADE CHICKEN STOCK

1 chicken carcass
2 T. garlic, minced
2 carrots, diced
Water as needed
2 stalks celery, diced
2 chicken bouillon cubes
2 onions (or 4 T. dried minced onions), diced
1 tsp. black pepper

Place the carcass, vegetables and garlic in a large cooking pot. Add enough water to cover the carcass. Dissolve bouillon cubes in one cup of water and add that plus the pepper to the pot. Bring to boil then reduce heat to low and cook for 8-10 hours. Add water as needed. Should make about 3 cups of chicken stock.

LASAGNA SOUP
4 garlic cloves, sliced
1 T. olive oil
10 large basil leaves, staked and chopped into shreds
8 oz. lean Italian sausage, about 3 links, casings removed
1 c. part-skim ricotta cheese
1/4 tsp. crushed red pepper
1/4 c. grated Parmesan
1 tsp. dried basil
2 T. chopped flat leaf parsley
1/4 tsp. dried oregano (optional)
32 oz. container chicken broth
1 c. cooked pasta, bow ties are
1 - 28oz can crushed tomatoes nice
1 tsp kosher salt
black pepper
Sauté the garlic in the olive oil, over medium high heat, in a large pot until fragrant, 2 to 4 minutes. Add the sausage and cook, breaking up with fork until browned and in fine pieces, 6 to 8 minutes. Add the crushed red pepper, basil, and oregano - cook for 1 additional minute, stirring constantly. Add the broth, tomatoes, salt and pepper. Bring to a boil, lower heat and simmer 15 to 20 minutes. Just before serving, add the cooked bow tie pasta and fresh basil. To serve. Blend the ricotta, 2 tablespoons Parmesan, and parsley in a small bowl. Ladle the soup into a shallow bowl, add a dollop of the ricotta mixture in the center, and sprinkle with additional Parmesan.

LEMON EGG SOUP
2 (10.75oz) cans condensed chicken broth
2 eggs
2 T. lemon juice
1 (8oz) pkg. non-fat cream cheese
1/2 tsp. grated lemon rind
1/2 c. rice (optional)
Bring broth to boil; add rice. Cover; simmer 20 minutes. Remove from heat. Combine softened cream cheese, eggs and lemon juice; mixing until well blended. Gradually add to broth; stirring constantly until smooth. Stir in lemon rind; heat thoroughly.
Note: Yield: 8 (1/2 c.) servings. Strain out the rice to enjoy during the liquid phase.

LOW CARB TOMATO GINGER CHICKEN NOODLE SOUP

I T. sesame oil
3/4 lb. boneless and skinless
I onion, diced chicken breast
I c. shredded carrots (or diced)
2 T. soy sauce
3 celery stalks, diced
12 oz. pkg Kelp noodles, rinsed
3 garlic cloves and cut into smaller pieces
2 T. tomato paste
2 T. Sriracha or Asian chile
2 T. grated ginger paste (optional)
8 c. chicken broth

Heat a large soup pot over medium heat with olive oil. When hot add the onions, carrots, celery, garlic, and ginger. Cook for 8-10 minutes until fragrant and veggies are beginning to soften. Stir in the tomato paste. Add the chicken and chicken broth. Cover and simmer for 15-20 minutes until chicken is cooked through. Remove chicken and shred it. Add it back to the pot along with the soy sauce a, kelp noodles, and Sriracha if you are using it. Let cook for 5 minutes or until kelp noodles are soft.

Note: Strain soup for liquid phase, blend for mushy phase. 115 calories, 3.6g of fat, 6.1g of carbohydrates, 1.5g of fiber, 14.2g of protein

MAMA'S POTATO SOUP
I lb bacon, cooked well done and crumbly
I c. milk or heavy whipping cream
8-10 medium potatoes, cubed
2-4 T. cornstarch mixed with 2 c. water
1/4 tsp. thyme
1/4 tsp. cilantro
I stick butter
1/2 tsp. chives
1/4 tsp. pepper
shredded cheddar cheese for garnish (optional)
salt to taste
sour cream for garnish (optional)
about 8 cups water
After the potatoes are cut up, add them to a cooking pot and fill the pot with the water. The water should cover the potatoes and have at least one inch of extra water on top of the potatoes. Bring to a boil and reduce heat but continue boiling for about an hour, stirring frequently. Add in butter and spices. Mix well. Add in salt to taste. Add in bacon and milk.
Return mixture to a boil. Reduce heat to simmer, and mix the cornstarch mixture. Add cornstarch mixture to pot. This should cause it to thicken. Let simmer until ready to serve. Garnish with shredded cheddar cheese and sour cream.
Note: Must be strained for liquid phase, blended for mushy phase. Very flavorful to break the same ole' same ole' in the early phases.

PUMPKIN BISQUE SOUP
2 c. puréed pumpkin
2 cloves garlic, minced
4 c. water
I onion, minced (optional)
I c. fat-free evaporated milk (or lactose free milk)
1/4 tsp. cinnamon
1/4 tsp. allspice
1/4 tsp ground nutmeg
Add all ingredients to a slow cooker and set on low for 8 hours. Use a blender or immersion blender to blend until smooth liquid. Enjoy.
Note: Calories: 110 Fat: .5g Carbs: 21g Fiber: 4g Protein: 7g

SLOW COOKER CHEESY CAULIFLOWER SOUP

I head cauliflower, cut into florets
1/4 c. flour (omit for low carb)
12oz fat free evaporated milk
I c. diced carrots
1/2 c. skim milk
I onion, diced
11/2 c. shredded reduced fat
3 celery stalks, diced
cheddar cheese
2 garlic cloves, diced
salt and pepper to taste
4 c. chicken or vegetable broth

Add the cauliflower, carrots, onion, celery, garlic, and broth to the crockpot. Cook on low for 4 hours or until veggies are soft. Stir together the flour, evaporated milk, and skim milk. Add to the slow cooker and turn it up to high for I hour. This will thicken up the soup. Season the soup with salt and pepper to taste. Use an immersion blender (or blend in batches) until smooth. Stir in the cheese until it melts completely.

Note: 230 calories, 6.8g of fat, 13.3g of carbohydrates, 1.7g of fiber, 31.4g of protein, Sugars: 7.8g

SLOW COOKER FRENCH ONION SOUP

4 large onions, thinly sliced
3 T. flour
1/2 T. butter
2 qts. beef stock or chicken
1/2 T. olive oil stock
1/2 tsp. sugar

Place the onions, butter, oil, sugar, and flour into a 4 qt. slow cooker. Cook on high for 40 minutes and then add the stock and reduce to low. Cook for 8 hours. Strain soup for liquid phase, do not strain for mushy phase.

Note: Calories: 140; Fat: 4.5g; Carbs: 19g; Protein: 7g

SLOW COOKER SPLIT PEA SOUP
I bag of green split peas
salt and pepper to taste
6-10 baby carrots, chopped finely or grated
I ham bone or ham pieces for flavoring
8 c. water
Place split peas in slow cooker and cover with water. Add carrots, salt, pepper and ham-bone. Cook on low for 8 - 10 hours. Remove ham-bone and using a hand mixer, blend the carrots and peas into a fine purée. Enjoy
Note: Calories: 230 Fat:1g Carbs 43g Fiber: 2g Protein: 16g

SPLIT PEA SOUP
1/2 c. green split peas
I tsp minced sage
1/2 c. yellow split peas
1/4 tsp dill weed
I large carrot, diced
1/4 tsp ground cayenne
I large parsnip, diced
I tsp hickory liquid smoke
I stalk celery, diced
1/2 tsp celery flakes
I medium onion, diced
5 c. water
2 shallots, minced
4 oz. 98% fat free ham steak, diced
Place all ingredients into a 4 quart slow cooker. Stir. Cook on low for 12-15 hours. If the soup is wetter than desired, uncover and cook on high for 30 minutes before serving. Use an immersion blender for mushy phase or strain soup for liquid phase.
Note: Calories: 230; Fat: 1g; Carbs: 43g; Protein: 16g

SWEET SOUP

2 qt. water 1 lb. prunes
1/2 c. tapioca
1 tsp. cinnamon (or cinnamon
1 c. raisins sticks)
4 T. vinegar
2 c. sweetened fruit juice*
11/2 c. granulated Splenda®

*You can use grape juice. Boil prunes and raisins together until well done. I hen add all other ingredients. Boil until tapioca is clear. Strain for liquid phase, purée for mushy phase.

TOMATO BASIL SOUP

1 T. butter
2 T. fresh chopped basil
1 lrg onion, diced
4 c. chicken broth
1 garlic clove, sliced
1 - 28oz can Italian Plum tomatoes in purée

Melt the butter in a large saucepan, over medium heat. Add the onion and garlic - cook until softened. Place the cooked vegetables and the tomatoes in a blender and blend until smooth. Pour the creamy tomato mixture back into the pot - stir in the basil and the chicken broth and bring to a boil. Simmer for 15 minutes. Serve with a swirl of about a tablespoon of half & half if desired.

VEGETABLE SOUP

Joan S.
1 large bag frozen mixed vegetables
1 large bottle tomato or V8 juice
pepper and salt to taste

Put all ingredients into a large pot and cook about an hour on medium to low heat. When vegetables are soft, remove from heat and using an immersion blender, blend soup until all vegetable chunks are liquid. Add water to thin, if desired. Enjoy.

VEGETABLE STOCK
3 medium to large carrots, 3 bell peppers, halved
peeled 2 shallots
3 parsnips, peeled (optional) I whole head of garlic or 2 T.
3 large onions, peeled and minced garlic
quartered 5 quarts of water
3 whole turnips I bunch of parsley
3 rutabagas, quartered I bunch of thyme
In a large cooking pot add water, vegetables and herbs. Cook on high until boiling, then turn down to low and simmer for 8 hours. Strain the stock and store it in your freezer until use or eat fresh.
Note: Calories: 100; Fat: 0g; Carbs: 24g; Protein:3g; Fiber: 5g;

Mushy Phase

BAKED POTATO SOUP
Carol Solen
I onion, sliced (or whole, peeled)
1/2 tsp pepper
1/4 c. cheddar cheese, shredded
4 russet potatoes, peeled and cubed
3 T. reduced fat sour cream
2 strips of bacon, cooked and crumbled
5 c. water
1/4 tsp. salt
Place onion, potatoes, water, salt and pepper in large cooking pot. Bring to a boil and continue cooking for approximately 20 minutes or until potatoes are extremely tender and fall apart upon touch. Purée using an immersion blender. Stir in remaining ingredients and enjoy.
Note: Calories: 170; Fat: 3.5g; Carbs: 28g; Protein: 6g; Fiber: 3g

CAULIFLOWER SOUP

I head cauliflower, cut in tiny pieces
2 c. milk
1/2 tsp. Worcestershire sauce
1/4 c. butter
3/4 tsp. salt
2/3 c. chopped onion
I c. grated Cheddar cheese
2 T. flour chopped parsley
2 c. chicken broth

Cook cauliflower in boiling, salted water until tender; drain. Reserve liquid. Melt butter; add onions and cook until soft. Blend in flour. Add broth and cook, stirring constantly, until mixture boils. Stir in I cup liquid from cauliflower, milk, Worcestershire sauce and salt. Add cauliflower; heat to boiling. Stir in cheese. Use immersion blender to purée soup. Sprinkle with parsley.

Note: Add a scoop of protein for an extra protein boost.

CLASSIC CHILI

I lb extra lean ground beef, browned, drained and rinsed
3 (15 oz) cans chili beans
I tsp. dried oregano
I c. chopped onions
Shredded cheddar cheese
1/2 c. chopped green peppers (optional)
2 c. water Sour cream (optional)
2 (8 oz) cans tomato sauce

In large pot, add beef, onions, green peppers, water, beans, tomato sauce and oregano. Bring to a boil. Reduce heat and simmer 30 minutes, covered. Top with cheese and sour cream.

EASY PEAZY CHILI

I (16 oz) can hot vegetable Juice
I lb. ground beef, browned, drained and rinsed
I (16 oz) can stewed tomatoes
I (16 oz) can kidney beans
I (16 oz) jar spaghetti sauce

Mix together all ingredients and simmer until ready to serve.

HAMBURGER VEGETABLE SOUP
Joan S.
1 lb. ground lean beef, browned, drained and rinsed
1 (10oz) can tomatoes with chiles (optional, gives it a little heat)
1 (29oz) can mixed vegetables, or bag of frozen similar vegetables
1/8 tsp. parsley
1/8 tsp thyme
2 (15oz) can petite diced tomatoes
salt and pepper to taste
Combine in large pot and cook on low for 30-60 minutes, depending on the desired consistency of the vegetables. Using an immersion blender, blend soup until creamy. Add water if needed to thin. Enjoy.

HEARTY MEXICAN GARLIC SOUP
3 whole heads of garlic
1 tsp. turmeric
3 T. oil
1/4 c. lime juice
1 lrg. onion, sliced thin
Sour cream or yogurt, to garnish
8 c. rich chicken stock
1 to 2 chipotle chilies, fresh, dried or canned
Sliced green onions, to garnish
Minced fresh cilantro, to garnish
1 tsp. cumin (or to taste)
Preheat oven to 400°. Separate the cloves of garlic. Arrange in a shallow pan; coat with 1 tablespoon oil. Bake about 45 minutes, until soft. Peel the cloves. Sauté the onions in 1 tablespoon oil; purée in a blender with the garlic adding 1/4 c. chicken stock. Heat remaining oil in a large saucepan; add to puréed mixture. Cook until it begins to dry out and brown lightly. Add stock, chipotles, cumin and turmeric; simmer 25 to 30 minutes. Add lime juice and pour into a serving bowl. Garnish with sour cream, green onions and cilantro.
Note: Yield: 6 to 8 servings.

SLOW COOKER BAKED POTATO SOUP
I onion, sliced (optional)
1/4 c. shredded sharp Cheddar
4 russet potatoes, peeled and cubed
3 T. reduced-fat sour cream
2 strips turkey bacon, cooked and crumbled
5 cups water
1/4 tsp. salt
1/3 c. diced green onion
1/2 tsp white pepper

Place the onions, potatoes, water, salt and pepper into a 4 qt. slow cooker. Cook on low for 7 hours. Purée using an immersion blender or purée in batches in a blender. Stir in cheese, sour cream, bacon crumbles, and green onion.

Note: Calories: 170; Fat: 3.5g; Carbs: 28g; Protein: 6g

SPAGHETTI SOUP
I 1/2 lb extra lean ground beef, browned, drained and rinsed
I lg jar spaghetti sauce
Garlic, minced or garlic salt
I onion, chopped
1/4 tsp crushed red pepper
I green pepper, chopped
2 T. sugar or Splenda®
I c. celery, chopped
I tsp. Italian seasoning
I c. carrots, chopped
8 oz cooked spaghetti
I to 1 1/2 qt. water
2 qt or 3 lg cans whole tomatoes

Boil water; add vegetables and simmer until well done. Break up tomatoes and add vegetables. Add spaghetti sauce, hamburger and spices, simmer. Add drained spaghetti, just before serving. Strain soup to have during liquid phase or purée during mushy phase.

Solid Phase

CROCKPOT CHICKEN AND DUMPLINGS
Dianna Gill
3-4 boneless, skinless chicken breasts
I small bag of frozen veggies (corn, peas, green beans, carrots)
I small can cream of celery
I small can cream of mushroom
I-2 cans of biscuit dough
I small can cream of chicken
salt and pepper to taste
I lrg box / can chicken broth
I bag of no yolk dumpling noodles
Place chicken breasts, veggies & broth in crock pot on high for 2-3 hours. Add all 3 creamed cans. Add 3/4 of bag of noodles (may need to add a cup or two of water at this point) cook for 1/2 hour or so. Cut each biscuits dough into four's & place into crock pot & stir. Cook for an additional 1/2 hour or so. Add salt & pepper.

STEAK SOUP
2 c. sirloin steak, grilled, leftover
I c. green beans, chopped
2 c. shredded cabbage
2 T. beef-flavored soup base, liquid or paste
1/2 c. dried pearl barley
1/2 c. dried lentils
3 c. water
1/2 c. dried split peas
I c. tomato juice
I T. dried crushed oregano
2 lrg. potatoes, peeled & diced
I tsp. garlic salt
3 lrg. carrots, peeled & diced
1/2 tsp. chili powder
2 stalks celery, diced
1/4 tsp. ground black pepper
I can diced tomatoes, with liquid
1/4 tsp. ground bay leaves
Dissolve beef-flavored soup base in 1 cup water; add steak pieces. Simmer for 15 minutes. Add all other remaining ingredients and bring to a boil; reduce heat and simmer for 2 to 3 hours. Add additional water or tomato juice as needed. Serve with a crusty bread.

SWISS VEGETABLE MEDLEY SOUP

1 (16oz) pkg of frozen mixed vegetables
1/4 tsp fresh ground pepper
1 (4oz) jar diced pimentos, drained (optional)
1 (10.75 oz) can cream of mushroom soup
1 (2.8 oz) can of french fried onions
1 c. shredded cheddar cheese (or more to taste)
1/3 c. fat free or low fat sour cream

Preheat oven to 350°. In large bowl, combine vegetables, soup, 1/2 c. cheese, sour cream, pepper, pimentos and 1/2 can french-friend onions. Pour into shallow 1-quart casserole dish. Bake, covered for 30 minutes or until vegetables are tender. Sprinkle remaining cheese and onion in diagonal row across top. Bake uncovered for 5 more minutes or until onions are golden brown.

VEGETABLE PASTA SALAD

8 oz. uncooked pasta
1/4 c. honey mustard
⅓ c. chopped onion
1/4 c. mayonnaise
1 c. chopped mushrooms
1/4 c. white vinegar
1 c. chopped cucumber (peeled)
1/2 tsp. salt
1 c. chopped broccoli florets
1/8 tsp. pepper
1/2 c. vegetable oil
2 c. shredded cheddar cheese

Cook pasta according to package directions bringing it to al dente. Rinse and drain well. Combine vegetables in large bowl. Whisk together oil, honey mustard, mayo, vinegar, salt and pepper. Add pasta to the vegetables and mix well. Add dressing and cheese and stir until well blended. Refrigerate 2 to 4 hours before serving. Add any additional vegetables as desired.

4 VEGETABLES AND SIDE DISHES

Mushy Phase

BEAN SPREAD
1 can (15 oz) pinto or kidney beans
Green or Red Tabasco sauce, to taste
Juice of 1 lime
salt (optional)
Mix all ingredients together and blend with hand mixer or food processor.
Note: Calories: 198 Fat: 1.5 grams Protein: 11.5 grams Carbs: 34.5 g

CAULIFLOWER MAC N' CHEESE
Jennifer and Sue at 7 Bites
1 head of cauliflower cut into bite sized pieces
3 tsp. brown mustard (or any mustard)
1 box chicken broth
1/8 tsp garlic powder
11/2 c. whole cream
1/4 tsp. cayenne pepper
4 oz. cream cheese
1/4 tsp. salt and pepper
2 c. shredded cheddar cheese
Cook cauliflower in chicken broth until soft. In a small saucepan, mix cream, cheeses, mustard, garlic powder, peppers and salt. Heat until cheese mixture is silky. Spray a baking dish with cooking spray. In a bowl, mix the cauliflower and the cheese mixture. Bake in the oven at 350° until slightly browned. Enjoy.

CAULIFLOWER MASHED "POTATOES"

Jennifer and Sue at 7 Bites
3 T. butter pinch of black pepper
I whole head cauliflower
I box of chicken broth
1/2 block cream cheese
5-6 potatoes
pinch of kosher salt

Cook cauliflower and diced potatoes in chicken broth. When potatoes are soft and cauliflower is soft, add cream cheese, salt and pepper. Mix all ingredients in food processor until well puréed. Transfer to oven dish and cook at 350° for about 15 minutes or until heated all the way through.

CHACE'S CAULIFLOWER MASH

I head cauliflower, rinsed, trimmed and cut into 2-3"
chunks
2 oz fat-free cream cheese
I oz grated fat-free or reduced fat cheese for garnish
1-2 shallots, sliced
salt and pepper to taste
2 tsp. olive oil
11/2 c. broth, chicken or vegetable

Sauté shallots in olive oil in a 4 qt. pan, until soft but not browned. Add cauliflower and broth, cover pan, reduce heat and simmer 10 minutes, until soft. Remove from heat and cool slightly (10-20 minutes.) Place cauliflower and cream cheese in blender. Do not fill blender more than 2/3 full! Cover with lid and purée until smooth. Carefully remove lid and add salt and pepper to taste. Divide into 4 servings and garnish with grated cheese.

Note: Calories: 110 Total Fat: 3.5g Carbs: 12g Protein: 8g

CHEESY HASHBROWN CASSEROLE

6-8 medium to large potatoes
salt and pepper to taste
I (16oz.) pkg low-fat cheddar cheese, divided
I (10.75oz) can low-sodium cream of chicken soup
I (8oz.) container fat free sour cream
Preheat oven to 350°. Slice potatoes in half and put in food processor on the shredding blade. Pour hashbrowns into large mixing bowl. Add remaining ingredients. Use cooking spray to coat a 13 x 9 inch pan. Cook for I hour. Add remaining cheese to top of casserole, cook an additional 20 minutes or until cheese is slightly browned. Serve hot.

CHEESY SCALLOPED POTATOES

I 1/2 c. skim milk non-stick cooking spray
2 T. flour 4 med. potatoes, peeled & thinly
1/2 tsp. salt or seasoned salt sliced
⅛ tsp black pepper 1/2 c. shredded cheese (or more
garlic powder (optional) to taste)
1/2 c. chopped onion Snipped fresh parsley
For sauce, in a small saucepan, stir together milk, flour, salt, pepper, and garlic powder, if desired. Cook and stir over medium heat until thickened and bubbly. Stir in onion. Spray a I 1/2 quart casserole dish with non-stick cooking spray. Place half of the potatoes in the dish. Top with half of the sauce. Repeat layers with remaining potatoes and sauce. Bake, covered, at 350° for 65 minutes, or until potatoes are tender, stirring once. Remove from oven and sprinkle with cheese. Cover and let stand I to 2 minutes, or until cheese is melted. If desired, garnish with parsley.
Note: Yield: 8 servings. Purée finished potatoes with immersion blender to enjoy while in the mushy phase.

GARLICKY BROCCOLI & RICOTTA

muschealth.com
4 c. broccoli (1 bunch)
1 c. fat-free ricotta cheese
Cooking spray
1 tsp. fresh ginger, grated
2 lg. cloves garlic (minced)
1/4 tsp. red pepper
Cut up broccoli into small pieces. Steam broccoli until soft, about 10-15 minutes. Coat a small nonstick skillet with cooking spray and sauté garlic over medium heat until barely golden. Drain broccoli, place in food processor with ricotta, garlic, and seasonings and pulse until combined
Note: Yields: 4 (1 cup) servings Calories: 88 Fat: 0.5g Protein: 13g

HIGH PROTEIN GARLIC MASHED POTATOES

11 red potatoes (large organic)
4 1/2 cloves garlic
3 1/4 c. navy beans (cooked, two 15-oz cans)
1 tsp sea salt
1/4 tsp paprika, ground
1/4 c. soy (free Earth Balance buttery spread)
ground black pepper to taste
herbs and seasoning to taste
almond milk (2 T. unsweet)
Wash potatoes with a potato scrubber, chop into large chunks, and toss into a large pot. I prefer to leave the skin on, but you can peel if desired. Fill pot with water until potatoes are covered. Cook on medium-high heat for about 30-35 minutes until fork tender. Drain potatoes and place in a large bowl. Drop in garlic cloves into a food processor (running) and process until finely chopped. Add drained and rinsed beans, salt, paprika, and process until mostly smooth. After cooling potatoes for a few minutes, take a potato masher and mash until desired consistency is achieved. Now add your milk and Earth Balance and keep mashing. Add processed bean mixture to potato mixture and mash until smooth. Sprinkle with black pepper, other herbs, and additional sea salt. Serve with Earth Balance, salsa, ketchup, or BBQ sauce, and a serving of cooked veggies to round out the meal. Note: You can also swap the beans for 1 cup of red lentils. Simply stir in cooked lentils as you mash the potatoes.
Note: Per serving, approx: 336 calories, 7g fat, 11g fiber, 11g protein,

MASHED CAULIFLOWER
Carla Harrison
1 bag frozen cauliflower florets
2 T. real bacon bits
3/4 c. fat free shredded cheddar
2/3 c. instant potato flakes or cheese buds (optional. see notes)
1/2 c half and half
1/4 c. butter or margarine
In a large, covered, microwavable dish, microwave cauliflower with about 2 tablespoons of water until MUSHY (about 25 minutes on high, stirring halfway through). Add all other ingredients and mash with a potato masher until you reach the desired consistency. If the cheese isn't completely melted, microwave again for 1 minute and mix well. If it's too thick, you can add a little water. Salt and pepper to taste.
Note: You can omit the potato flakes or reduce the amount to lower the carb count, but they really make a difference in the texture

QUINOA (KEEN-WAH) TABOULI
muschealth.com
2 c. water
2 T. fresh mint
1/2 c. fresh lemon juice
11/2 c. fresh parsley, coarsely
1 c. quinoa chopped
1/3 c. olive oil
1 c. scallions, chopped
3 medium ripe tomatoes
salt to taste
Place quinoa in a colander and rinse several times rubbing the grains to remove the bitter outer layer. Place water and quinoa into a 2-quart saucepan. Bring to a boil. Reduce heat to a simmer and cover. Cook for 10 to 15 minutes or until all the water has been absorbed. While the quinoa is cooking, finely chop the tomatoes, mint, parsley and scallions. Add lemon juice and olive oil to tomato mixture. Stir in cooked quinoa and salt. Mix well. Let tabouli sit in the refrigerator for overnight to blend flavors. Tabouli is traditionally served at room temperature so removed from fridge 30-60 minutes before serving.
Note: Yields: 6 servings Calories: 240 Fat: 13 g Protein: 5 g

SOUTHWEST MAC N' CHEESE
16oz wagon wheel pasta
11/4 c. shredded Cheddar cheese
1 jar (15oz) Cheez Whiz®
2 scallions, chopped
11/2 c. skim milk
2 tsp. dry Southwest seasoning
Preheat oven to 350°. Coat shallow 2 qt. casserole dish with cooking spray. Cook pasta according to package directions. Drain well; return to pot. Meanwhile, in small pot over medium heat, combine Cheez Whiz®, milk and 1 cup grated cheese; cook, stirring until heated through and grated cheese melts. Stir in scallions and seasoning until blended. Stir cheese sauce into pasta until completely coated. Transfer pasta mixture to casserole dish. Sprinkle remaining cheese on top of mixture. Bake 25-30 minutes or until heat through.
Note: Servings: 8; Calories: 400; Fat: 15g; Carbs: 50g; Protein: 20g

SPINACH GARLIC YOGURT DIP
3 T. olive oil
2 garlic cloves, minced
2 - 11oz pkgs fresh baby spinach or 1 - 10oz pkg frozen chopped spinach, thawed and squeezed dry
11/2 c. plain Greek yogurt
1/2 c. chopped fresh cilantro
1/2 tsp. salt
1/4 tsp. black pepper
Heat 1 tablespoon oil in a large skillet over high heat, add the spinach and toss until just wilted. Transfer to a colander to drain and cool. Squeeze spinach to remove excess liquid and finely chop.Combine chopped spinach, olive oil, garlic, yogurt, cilantro, salt, and pepper. Add additional salt and pepper to taste. Cover and chill before serving.

STUFFED BAKED POTATOES
Tammy McCoy
4 lrg baking potatoes
1/2 tsp. salt
8 slices bacon (optional)
1/2 tsp. pepper
1 c. fat-free or low fat sour cream divided
1 c. shredded cheddar cheese,
1/2 cup milk green onions, sliced, divided
4 T. butter or margarine (optional)
Wash your potatoes and then poke at the skin with a fork to allow steam to escape. Bake potatoes in the oven for an hour at 350°F or 175°C. While the potatoes are cooking, cook up the 8 strips of bacon in a pan. When they are cooked, drain them and let them cool on a paper towel. Now break them up into small pieces with your hands and set aside. When the potatoes are fully cooked, take them out and slice them in half lengthwise. Now scoop out the potato flesh into a bowl. If the potatoes have been fully cooked, this should be easy. Don't worry too much about getting all the flesh out. If you do that you could easily rip the skin apart and we want it intact. Mix the potato flesh with the sour cream, milk, butter, salt, pepper, half of the cheese, and half of the green onions. In other words, set aside one half of the cheese and one half of the green onions and toss everything else in with the potato flesh and mix it up. When it's all smooth and thoroughly mixed, spoon the mixture back into the potato skins. Sprinkle the remaining bacon, cheese, and green onions on top of the potatoes. Put the potatoes back into the oven at 350°F/175°C for another 15 minutes.

SUGAR-FREE CRANBERRY SAUCE
1 bag of fresh or frozen whole cranberries
Pinch of ground cinnamon
1/2 - 1 c. Splenda® granular
1 orange, unpeeled and cut into quarters
Cook cranberries, orange pieces, and cinnamon in 1/2 cup water in a medium saucepan over medium heat until berries pop. Turn down heat and simmer until berries are soft, and mixture is deep red and thickened, 20-25 minutes. Remove from heat, and stir in Splenda. Cool mixture and chill up to 3 days before serving. If a smooth cranberry sauce is preferred, remove orange pieces then purée mixture in food processor or blender before chilling.
Note: Calories: 15 Protein: 0g Carbs: 4g Fiber: 1g

SUPER VEGGIE CASSEROLE

20 oz. Californian vegetables, thawed
8 oz. Cheese Whiz®
1 stick margarine or butter
1 c. quick cooking rice
1/3 c. milk
Onion flakes
1/4 c. water
1 can cream of chicken soup

Place vegetables into a casserole pan and sprinkle on the rice and onion. Heat the remaining ingredients in a saucepan and stir until they are well blended. Pour the mixture over the vegetables and bake at 325° for 1 hour. Use immersion blender to make consistency mushy.

SWEET POTATO CASSEROLE

Dianna Gill

2 lrg cans of sweet potatoes 3 T. flour
1/4 tsp. salt 3/4 c. light brown sugar
1/4 c. butter or margarine (twice) 1 bag chopped pecans
2 eggs (optional)
1 tsp. vanilla dash of cinnamon
1/2 c. white sugar or Splenda® miniature marshmallows
2 T. heavy cream (optional)

In large bowl mix together the following: (use mixer) Sweet potatoes, salt, butter, eggs, vanilla, white sugar, heavy cream & transfer to 9 X 13 dish. Add layer of miniature marshmallows & sprinkle with cinnamon.

In medium bowl mix together:Butter, flour, brown sugar and chopped pecans. Sprinkle over the sweet potato mixture. Bake for 30 minutes or until topping is crisp and lightly browned.

TACO REFRIED BEANS WITH CHEESE

Amy Solen

1 lrg can refried beans
2-3 oz. shredded Mexican cheese
1 packet taco seasoning

Put refried beans in a microwave safe bowl and heat in microwave for 1 to two minutes. Stir thoroughly and heat for an additional minute or until hot throughout. Add 1/2 packet taco seasoning to beans. Mix well. Add cheese to top of mixture and microwave until cheese is melted.

Solid Phase

AUTHENTIC PORK LO-MEIN NOODLES
1/2 lb fresh pork tenderloin
Meat Marinade:
2 tsp. cornstarch
I tsp. sugar
I tsp. soy sauce
I tsp. rice wine
Sauce Mixture:
4 tsp. cornstarch
I c. chicken broth
2 T. oyster sauce
2 garlic cloves, crushed
1/4 tsp. ginger
4 T. peanut oil
Vegetables:
I T. fresh ginger, cut very fine
5-6 large mixed mushrooms
1/2 c. bamboo shoot
I red bell pepper or I carrot
I sm. onion, cut into wedges
2 green onions, shredded
I medium zucchini or I medium celery, cut in I-inch strips
Seasoning in Noodles:
I lb fresh Chinese egg noodles
2 T. peanut oil
I T. sesame oil
2 T. oyster sauce or soy sauce
I 1/2 T. soy sauce
I 1/2 tsp. rice vinegar

Cut pork into thin strips, and then into pieces. Mix with meat marinade for 30 minutes. Slice mushrooms, bamboo shoots, red pepper and zucchini into thin strips. Mix sauce. Parboil noodles for 3 minutes. Rinse and drain. Bring another pot of water to boil, and keep hot. Heat 2 T. oil in wok. Stir fry all vegetables together for 2-3 minutes. Sprinkle on a little salt and I teaspoons of sugar. Set aside. Add 2 T. oil, and stir fry pork until done. Add sauce mixture. Stir until thickened. Add the vegetables. Stir until well mixed. Put noodles into hot pot of water for 10-15 seconds, just to heat. Drain. Put back in pot, and add seasonings to noodles. Serve meat and vegetables over noodles. Not a low calorie food!!!

Note: Calories: 1588; Total Fat: 63g; Carbs: 192g; Protein: 64g

BROCCOLI EGG AND CHEESE BAKE

6 large eggs
1 tsp. salt
4 oz light margarine
1 dash black pepper
1/2 lb low fat cheddar cheese
1 dash paprika (optional)
6 T. flour
4 oz. jar chopped pimento
2 lbs. nonfat cottage cheese (optional)
10 oz. frozen, chopped broccoli, thawed
1/2 c. sliced mushrooms, fresh or canned (optional)

Preheat oven to 350°. Combine all ingredients. Spray 2-quart casserole dish with cooking spray. Place combined ingredients in prepared pan and bake for 90 minutes. Serve hot

Note: Calories: 115Fat: 5 grams Protein: 12 grams Carbs: 5g

FRIED CABBAGE DISH

Carla Harrison

1 lb bacon, finely chopped
1/4 tsp red pepper flakes
1 medium onion, chopped
1/2 tsp salt
2 lbs cabbage, finely diced
1/2 tsp black pepper

Fry bacon until crisp and well browned. Drain and set aside. Add chopped onion to the bacon grease and stir until translucent. Add cabbage, pepper flakes, salt and pepper, stirring until all cabbage is coated. Add the crumbled bacon bits and cover. Cook over low heat until cabbage is tender.

KRAUT CASSEROLE

1 (16oz) can of sauerkraut
1/2 c. mayonnaise
1 (16oz) can corned beef
3 eggs
3/4 c. biscuit mix
1 (11/4oz) pkg. Swiss cheese,
3/4 c. milk sliced

In a 9x13 inch baking dish, spread sauerkraut onto bottom, and top with the corned beef. Combine biscuit mix, milk, mayonnaise and eggs. Pour over corned beef. Arrange the cheese slices over the batter. Bake at 400° for 30 to 35 minutes.

LOW CARB GRILLED ZUCCHINI PIZZA

Large Zucchini slices, 3/4 inch thick
pizza toppings
low-fat pizza cheese (mozzarella pizza sauce or a blend)
Oil the grill grates, then preheat grill to medium-high. Cut zucchini
into thick slices about 3/4 inch thick. Grill the zucchini 7-8 minutes, or
until there are some grill marks and it's starting to be tender. If
desired, you can heat the sauce while the zucchini grills. Remove
zucchini from the grill, putting them grilled-side up on a cutting board
you can use to take them to the kitchen. Add sauce, cheese, and other
toppings as desired. Put loaded zucchini slices back on the grill and
cook 7-8 minutes more with the grill lid closed. Check them every few
minutes to see when the cheese is melted and the toppings are lightly
browned, especially if you're using a broiler. Remove zucchini pizzas
from grill and serve hot.

LOW CARB ZUCCHINI OVEN CHIPS

Carla Harrison
1/4 c. ground almonds or pecans
2 T. fat-free milk (or milk substitute)
1/4 c. grated fresh Parmesan cheese
2 1/2 c. (1/4 inch-thick) slices
1/4 t. seasoned salt zucchini (about 2 small)
1/4 t. garlic powder
non-stick cooking spray
1/8 t. black pepper
Preheat oven to 425. Combine first 5 ingredients in a medium bowl,
stirring with a whisk. Place milk in a shallow bowl. Dip zucchini slices
in milk, and dredge in dry mixture. Place coated slices on an oven
proof wire rack coated with cooking spray; place rack on a baking
sheet. Bake at 425 for 30 minutes or until browned and crisp. Serve
immediately.
Note: Makes 4 servings.

SPICY SWEET POTATO FRIES

I large or 2 medium sweet potatoes, sliced into
matchsticks (2 cups)
1/2 tsp. salt
1/2 tsp. pepper
1/2 tsp. chili powder
2 egg whites
1/4 tsp. cinnamon

Preheat the oven to 400 degrees. Cover a baking sheet with foil and spray with cooking spray. Beat the egg whites. Toss with the sweet potatoes and let all excess drain off. Lay out flat on the baking sheet, without having them overlap. Sprinkle with spices. Bake for 12 minutes. Flip over and bake for an additional 10 minutes.
Note: 98 calories, .2g of fat, 21.5g of carbs, 3g of fiber, 3.3g of protein

SUNRISE CARROTS

1 1/4 lb carrots
1/2 c. orange juice
2 T. sugar
1/2 tsp. ground ginger
2 tsp. cornstarch
4 T. butter
1/2 tsp. salt
I tsp. lemon rind (optional)

Slice carrots diagonally; cook until tender, about 20 minutes. Drain. Make sauce by combining dry ingredients. Add orange juice, butter and lemon rind. Cook over medium heat, stirring until thickened. Pour over carrots. Purée for mushy stage.

VEGETABLE TIAN
(Thinly sliced veggies, topped with cheese then roasted)
Tammy McCoy

1 T. olive oil
1 medium potato
1 medium onion
1 medium tomato
1 tsp. minced garlic
1 tsp. dried thyme
1 medium zucchini
salt and pepper to taste
1 medium yellow squash
1 c. shredded Italian cheese

Preheat the oven to 400°. Finely dice the onion and mince the garlic. Sauté both in a skillet with olive oil until softened (about five minutes). While the onion and garlic are sautéing, thinly slice the rest of the vegetables. Spray the inside of an 8x8 square or round baking dish with non-stick spray. Spread the softened onion and garlic in the bottom of the dish. Place the thinly sliced vegetables in the baking dish vertically, in an alternating pattern. Sprinkle generously with salt, pepper, and thyme. Cover the dish with foil and bake for 30 minutes. Remove the foil, top with cheese and bake for another 15-20 minutes or until the cheese is golden brown.

5 MAIN DISHES

Liquid Phase

CREAMY ALFREDO SAUCE

4 T. fat free margarine
I c. grated Parmesan cheese
I c. fat-free sour cream
pinch of ground nutmeg
1/4 c. egg substitute
salt and pepper to taste

Melt margarine over medium heat. Add sour cream. Reduce heat to low and whisk until margarine is incorporated into sour cream. Add egg substitute and continue to whisk (if heat is too high eggs will scramble!!!)When completely mixed, add cheese and continue stirring until cheese is melted into mixture. Remove from heat. Add nutmeg and season to taste

Note: Calories: 105 Fat: 4 grams Protein: 8 grams Carbohydrate: 7 grams Cholesterol: 14 mg Sodium: 387 mg Sugar: 4 grams

Mushy Phase

BEEF STEW WITH VEGGIES
2 lbs stew meat
1 can Italian cut green beans
5-6 red potatoes, cubed into bite size pieces
1 small onion, peeled
1-2 pkts Pioneer® brown gravy
2 pkts beef stew seasoning mix (one pkt makes 2 cups)
1 (16oz) bag peeled baby carrots
Place meat, potatoes, carrots, beans and onion (not cut) into slow cooker. (Onion can be diced, if so desired) Cook on High heat for 6-8 hours or until vegetables can be easily smashed with a spoon or fork. Meat will also easily fall apart. Whisk in one packet of Pioneer gravy to thicken stew. If too thin, add another packet of gravy. Serve.
Note: This is listed in the mushy phase because the solid food portions are cooked down to a mushy consistency. Also, the fresh vegetables can be replaced with 2 large cans of mixed vegetables.

CHEESY EGGS BAKE
6 large eggs, beaten
1 c. low-fat cottage cheese
1/4 c. flour (optional)
1 tsp baking powder
4 oz. (T.) light cream cheese,
⅛ tsp salt and pepper cubed
1/2 tsp. Italian seasoning
1 c. cubed low fat cheddar
1 c. skim milk cheese
Preheat oven to 350°. Spray 9x9 inch pan with vegetable cooking spray and set aside. In a large bowl, beat eggs until frothy. Whisk in flour, baking powder, salt, pepper, seasoning, milk, and cottage cheese. Stir in cubed cheeses. Pour into prepared pan. Bake for 30 - 35 minutes or until puffed, golden and set.
Note: Servings Per Recipe: 6 Calories: 215.3 Total Fat: 11.3 g Carbs: 9.2 g Protein: 19.0 g

CRUSTLESS SPINACH AND CHEESE QUICHE

muschealth.com
Butter flavored cooking spray
1 T. water
3/4 c. fresh white mushrooms
1/4 c. egg substitute
(chopped)
1/2 c. skim milk
1/4 c. shallots (chopped)
1/2 c. low-fat swiss cheese
2 (10 oz) pkgs frozen chopped (diced) spinach
1/4 tsp. ground nutmeg

Spray microwavable casserole dish with butter-flavored cooking spray. Chop mushrooms and shallots and add to dish, cover, and microwave on HIGH for 1 minute. Place frozen spinach and water on top of mushroom mixture. Cover, and microwave on high for 3 1/2 minutes. Remove from microwave and drain if too much liquid remains. In a separate bowl, combine egg substitute and milk, stir in diced cheese and nutmeg. Stir spinach, mushrooms and shallots to combine; pour egg/milk/cheese mixture on top, cover, and microwave on high for 4 minutes. Let cool and slice in squares.

Note: Yields: 4 (1 cup) servings Calories: 143 Fat: 4 g Protein: 15 g

EASY CHICKEN POT PIE

Shawn McCoy
2 c. chicken, cooked and finely chopped
1 c. milk
10 oz tube refrigerated biscuits
15 oz can mixed vegetables, drained
2 10 oz cans cream of chicken soup (or 1 chicken and 1 potato)

Combine first four ingredients together, placing an ungreased 3 quart casserole dish. Bake at 400° degrees F for 20 minutes. While baking, slice biscuits into quarters and set aside. Remove casserole dish from oven and stir.5. Arrange biscuit pieces on top of the chicken mixture; bake until golden (about 15 minutes).

Note: Makes 6 servings.

HARVEST CHILI
I can light red kidney beans
I tsp. pepper
I can red beans
I can dark red kidney beans
I can black beans
2 cans chili hot beans
2 pkts chili seasoning
I lb. ground beef (or turkey), browned and drained
I can great northern beans
I can pinto beans
saltines (optional)
low - fat shredded cheddar cheese (optional)
fat free sour cream (optional)

Empty all beans into crock pot, with juices. Add ground meat. Add pepper and chili seasoning. Mix well. Cook on medium for 6 - 8 hours. Stirring occasionally. Serve with cheese, sour cream and saltines.

JENNIE'S SPAGHETTI-LESS SPAGHETTI
Jennie at muschealth.com
1/2 c. frozen, chopped spinach, thawed
I c. fat-free ricotta cheese
2 T. grated Parmesan cheese
1/2 c. marinara sauce

Mix first 3 ingredients. Sprinkle Parmesan cheese on top. Microwave until melted, about 2 minutes.

Note: Yields I serving. Calories: 70 Fat: 4g Carbs: 4g Protein: 5g

JEN'S FUN CHILI

Jennifer and Sue at 7 Bites

2 lbs lean ground beef
2 tsp. salt, cumin, paprika, garlic powder, onion powder and oregano
1 medium onion, chopped
2 cloves garlic, minced
1 (6 oz.) can tomato paste
1/2 tsp. red pepper flake (or to taste)
1 (28 oz.) can crushed tomatoes
12 oz beer
1 T. brown sugar substitute
1/4 c. chili powder
2 tsp. cinnamon
1 tsp. ground black pepper

Stovetop directions: Brown ground beef with onions and garlic until no longer pink and onions are tender. Add all remaining ingredients and mix well. Bring to a bubble over medium high heat, then turn to medium low and simmer for up to 2 1/2 hours, stirring occasionally. If it looks like the liquid is evaporating too quickly, add some broth or more beer (water will dilute the flavor!). Slow cooker directions: Brown ground beef with onions and garlic until no longer pink and onions are tender. Combine remaining ingredients in slow cooker and mix well to combine. Add meat mixture and stir well to combine. Cook on low up to 12 hours or on high up to 8 hours. If it looks like it needs more liquid after a few hours, add more beer or add some beef broth (water will dilute the flavor!) Variations: *Use allspice instead of cinnamon! *Add 1/2 a block of Mexican chocolate! *Add 1 chopped bell pepper. *Use diced tomatoes instead of crushed tomatoes (2 cans) *Toss some chipotles or some dried chilis in!
Note: Nutrition per 1/2 C serving: Calories: 186 Carbs: 13g Protein: 18g

JIM'S EGG SALAD

Jim at muschealth.com
5 hard boiled eggs, finely chopped
1/4 cup finely chopped sweet onion
1/4 c. fat-free mayonnaise
Salt substitute and pepper to taste
⅛ c. fat-free Miracle Whip®
1 T. pickle relish (squeeze excess moisture through
sieve first and discard liquid)
Mix everything well and place in plastic container in fridge. This mixture basically yields about six-8 1/4 cup servings.
Note: Calories: 100 Fat: 2g Carbs: 10g Fiber: 1g Protein: 7g

JIM'S SWEET POTATOES

Jim at muschealth.com
2 medium sized sweet potatoes (or 1 large can)
1/4 tsp. cinnamon
1/4 tsp nutmeg
2 T. margarine
Peel and cube sweet potatoes (drain if using canned). Boil potatoes in water until soft; drain water. Add margarine, cinnamon and nutmeg to hot potatoes. Mix well with hand mixer until smooth.
Note: Yields: 8 servings, 1/4 cup each Calories: 50 Fat: 3 g Protein: 1 g Carb: 7 g (1 g fiber)

JOANN'S FAMILY CASSEROLE

Joann at muschealth.com
2 boneless, skinless chicken breasts
I c. I% cheddar cheese, finely shredded, divided
I can fat free cream of celery soup
1/2 small box spaghetti or any left over noodles
I (14oz) can artichoke, drained and diced
Preheat oven to 350-degrees. Spray a 9 x 9 casserole dish with cooking spray. Boil chicken in water for 30 minutes, remove (do not throw out water) & let cool enough to handle and shred. In a large mixing box, mix together the soup, artichoke and 1/2 the cheese. Add a little chicken broth to make smoother if needed. You want the mixture about as thick as creamed soup. Cook spaghetti or noodles in water from chicken (if not enough add chicken broth). Drain but don't rinse. Purée 2 oz. of shredded chicken. Using a spoon, mix chicken with 1/2 cup of soup mixture. Put this in your casserole dish in the corner. This part is for you only. Drop the spaghetti and rest of shredded chicken into the soup mixture; mix well, until coated, turn into casserole dish (try to keep your portion intact). Sprinkle top with remaining cheddar, make sure to cover yours also. Cover with foil and bake for 45 minutes, removing foil for last 5 minutes. Broil for 2-3 minutes on high. The cheese becomes golden brown. Let rest for about 10 minutes, it will be hot. Leftovers freeze well.
Note: Yields: Two 1/2 cup portions of pasta-free casserole (I" square each) Calories: 100 Fat: 2.5 g Protein: 11 g Carb: 7 g

JULIA'S PURÉED HEUVOES RANCHEROS

Julia at muschealth.com
1/3 c. fat free refried beans
I tsp. cottage cheese
1/8 c. egg substitute
I or 2 T. salsa
Spread refried beans in microwaveable small bowl, making a well in the middle. Put eggs in well, top with cottage cheese and spoon salsa around. Microwave 1 minute and stir eggs and cheese mixture. Microwave another minute.
Note: Yields:1 serving Calories: 90 Fat: 0 g Protein: 8 g Carb: 12 g (4 g fiber)

JULIE'S NO PASTA LASAGNA

Julie at muschealth.com
I small eggplant
1/2 can (12 oz) spaghetti sauce
1/2 c. vegetable broth
4 oz. extra lean ground beef
15oz. container fat free ricotta cheese
I egg
I tsp. salt
11/2 c. fat free shredded mozzarella cheese
I tsp. pepper
1/2 tsp. nutmeg

Peel the eggplant and cut into pieces 1/2 to ⅜ inch slices. Place the slices in a glass baking dish with 1/2 c. vegetable broth. Bake at 375o until tender. Place on paper towels and pat dry. Combine the spaghetti sauce and ground beef. Thoroughly mix ricotta, egg, salt, pepper, and nutmeg. Coat 9x9 baking dish with cooking spray. Layer the ingredients in the pan twice; first sauce, then ricotta, then eggplant, then mozzarella (and repeat). Bake at 350° for about 20 minutes or until mozzarella on top starts to brown. Can be puréed for mushy stage of diet.

Note: Yields: 8 servings Calories: 140 Fat: 2g Protein: 16g Carb: 14g
Some Healthy Substitutions: Try using 1/4 c. Egg Beaters
instead of 1 egg. If you can't find fat free ricotta cheese, try using fat free cottage cheese or 0% Greek strained yogurt.

SAVORY SALMON PATTIES

Joan S.

2 cans (6.5oz) salmon, drained and flaked
I lrg yellow onion, finely chopped
I c. mashed potatoes
1/2 tsp. paprika
2 T. plain low-fat yogurt
I T. lemon juice
2 T. prepared yellow mustard
1/2 c. fine dry bread crumbs
I lrg egg white
I 1/2 T. corn oil or vegetable oil
I medium carrot, peeled and finely chopped

In a medium-size bowl, combine the salmon, potatoes, yogurt, mustard, egg white, carrot, onion, paprika and lemon juice; shape into 8 patties. Put the bread crumbs on a plate and coat the patties with the crumbs. In a heavy 12inch skillet, heat the oil over moderate heat for I minute; add the patties and cook about 3 minutes on each side or until golden brown. Transfer to heated platter. Enjoy.

Solid Phase

BBQ ROASTED SALMON

1/4 c. pineapple juice
2 tsp. grated lemon rind
2 T. fresh lemon juice
3/4 tsp. ground cumin
4 salmon fillets (6 oz. each)
1/2 tsp. salt
2 T. brown sugar
1/4 tsp. cinnamon
4 tsp. chili powder

Preheat oven to 400 degrees. Combine first three ingredients in Ziploc bag. Marinate in refrigerator for one hour, turning occasionally. Remove salmon from bag and discard marinade. Combine remainder of ingredients and rub over fish. Place fillets in baking dish coated with cooking spray. Bake for 12-15 minutes or until desired doneness. Serve with lemon slice garnish.

Note: Calories: 225Fat: 6 grams Protein: 34 grams Carbohydrate: 7 grams

BEAN CASSEROLE FOR ONE
1/2 lb hamburger
1 tsp. salt
1/2 lb bacon
1 T. salad mustard
1 c. onion, diced
1/4 c. sweetener (or sugar)
1/2 c. ketchup
1 can Lima beans
1/2 c. brown sugar (or brown sugar substitute)
1 can kidney beans
1 can pork & beans
2 T. vinegar
1 can butter beans

Brown together hamburger, bacon and diced onion. Drain beans and add to hamburger mixture. Add remaining ingredients; mix well. Place into casserole dish and bake at 300° for 11/2 hours.
Note: If puréed with a blender or immersion blender, can be used in the purée stage.

BEEF N BEAN TACO SKILLET
1 lb ground beef
1/2 c. salsa, mild or spicy
1 pkt taco seasoning
1/4 c. water
1 can (16oz) pinto beans
1/2 c. Cheddar cheese, shredded
1 can condensed tomato soup
6 6-in. flour tortillas

In 10-inch skillet, cook beef over medium-high heat until crumbly and well-browned. Drain excess fat and rinse. Stir taco seasoning into beef; add beans, soup, salsa, and water. Reduce heat to low; simmer 10 minutes, stirring occasionally. Top with cheese and serve with tortillas. Refrigerate any leftovers.
Note: Makes 6 servings.

BIG-TIME BURGER

1 Boca Burger (Savory mushroom mozzarella flavor; found in grocer's freezer)
1 T. ketchup
1 T. mustard
Lettuce
1 hamburger bun
Tomato
1 T. light Miracle Whip or fat free mayonnaise
Onion, sliced

Prepare Boca Burger as directed on package. Put burger on bun with light miracle whip, ketchup, lettuce, tomato, and onion.
Note: Calories: 260 Fat: 5.5g Protein: 18 g Carbs: 40g

BROCCOLI & SPINACH STUFFED CHICKEN BREAST

Carla Harrison
1 pkg chopped spinach, thawed and patted dry
5 cloves garlic, minced or to taste
1 pkg chopped broccoli, thawed
2 lbs boneless, skinless chicken breasts or tenderloins, pounded to 1/4inch thickness
6 oz cream cheese, softened
1/2 c. shredded Mozzarella cheese
2 T. olive oil
3 lrg scallions, chopped

Preheat oven to 450°. Chop garlic and sauté in olive oil. Add spinach and broccoli and sauté until warm throughout. Take off heat and add cream cheese, mozzarella, chopped scallions, salt and pepper to taste. Take chicken and place a few spoonfuls of spinach mixture on chicken. Roll chicken around mixture and place in baking dish with ends facing down. Lie each piece right next to each other so it doesn't ooze out as it cooks. Any leftover filling can be added to pan to cook. Sprinkle more mozzarella on top, or spread mustard across the top of each chicken piece. Cook for 20 minutes covered, then uncover until chicken is fully cooked and reaches an internal temperature of at least 165°.

BUTTERMILK MARINATED CHICKEN BREASTS

1 c. buttermilk
1/2 tsp dried marjoram
1 T. Dijon mustard
1/2 tsp pepper
1 T. honey
1 tsp salt
1 T. fresh rosemary, chopped
8 split boneless, skinless chicken breasts
1/2 tsp dried thyme
1/2 tsp dried sage

Mix buttermilk, mustard, honey, and seasonings.Place chicken breasts in a freezer bag.Pour marinade over chicken breasts.*Grill over medium heat until chicken is tender and juices run clear.*Recipe can be frozen at this step. To cook, just thaw chicken and grill.Number of Servings: 8

Note: CALORIES: 282.8 | FAT: 3.2g | PROTEIN: 55.6g | CARBS: 3.9g

CAJUN CHICKEN AND DUMPLINGS

1 T. canola oil
1/2 tsp dried dill weed
1 onion, chopped
1/2 tsp ground cayenne
3 cloves garlic, minced
6 c. chicken stock (see recipe)
1 c. diced crimini mushrooms
3 c. diced, cooked chicken
2 carrots, diced breast
2 stalks celery, diced
1 T. baking powder
1 parsnip, diced
2 c. flour
1 jalapeño, seeded and diced
3/4 c. milk or fat-free buttermilk
1/2 tsp. salt
2 eggs
1/2 tsp. ground pepper
1/4 c. chopped green onion
1 lrg red skin potato, diced

Heat the canola oil in a skillet, then add the onions, garlic, and mushrooms. Sauté until softened, about 2 minutes. Add to a large slow cooker along with carrots, celery, parsnip, jalapeño, salt, pepper, potato, dill weed, cayenne, and stock. Cook on low for 6 hours. Add the cooked chicken and turn to high. Meanwhile, whisk the baking powder and flour in a medium bowl. Stir in the buttermilk, eggs and green onion. Mix to combine. Divide the mixture into 3" dumplings. Carefully drop the dumplings one at a time into the slow cooker. Cover and continue to cook on high for 30 minutes or until the dumplings are cooked through and fluffy.

Note: Calories: 490| Fat: 10g | Carbs: 63g | Protein: 36g

CAJUN CHICKEN STUFFED WITH PEPPER JACK CHEESE AND SPINACH

1 lb (16oz.) boneless, skinless chicken breast
2 tsp. olive oil
2 T. cajun seasoning
3 oz. reduced fat pepper jack cheese, shredded
1 T. bread crumbs
Toothpicks
1 c. frozen spinach, thawed and drained (or fresh cooked)
Preheat oven to 350°. Flatten the chicken to 1/4-inch thickness. In a medium bowl, combine the pepper jack cheese, spinach, salt and pepper. Combine the Cajun seasoning and breadcrumbs together in a small bowl. Spoon about 1/4 c of the spinach mixture onto each chicken breast. Roll each chicken breast tightly and fasten the seams with several toothpicks. Brush each chicken breast with the olive oil. Sprinkle the Cajun seasoning mixture evenly over all. Sprinkle any remaining spinach and cheese on top of chicken (optional).Place the chicken seam-side up onto a tin foil-lined baking sheet (for easy cleanup).Bake for 35 to 40 minutes, or until chicken is cooked through. Remove the toothpicks before serving. Count to make sure you have removed every last toothpick. Serve whole or slice into medallions.
Note: 1 serving (4 servings per recipe) Calories: 241 Total Fat: 9.7g Total Carbohydrates: 2g Dietary Fiber: 1g Sugars: 0g Total Protein: 32g

CARIBBEAN PULLED PORK

2 lbs pork loin
1/2 tsp ground cloves
1/4 c. chili sauce
1/2 tsp cayenne pepper
1 Scotch bonnet pepper, minced
1/2 tsp. oregano
1/4 c. red wine vinegar
1/2 tsp cumin
1/2 tsp. black pepper
1/2 tsp thyme
1 T. ginger preserves
1 tsp hickory liquid smoke
2 T. orange juice
1 onion, chopped
1 T. lime juice
2 cloves garlic
1/2 tsp allspice

Place all ingredients into a slow cooker. Cook on low for 8-10 hours or until the pork is easily shredded with a fork. Remove the pork from the slow cooker and place it on a plate. Shred it with a fork. Mash the mixture in the slow cooker with a potato masher or use an immersion blender. Return the pork to the slow cooker and toss to coat.

Note: Calories: 340 | Fat: 12g | Carbs: 7g | Protein: 46g

CHEESY VEGETARIAN CHILI

2 garlic cloves
2 T. chili powder
2 tsp olive oil
1 medium zucchini sliced thin
1 lrg green bell pepper, diced
2 - 15oz. cans red kidney beans,
1 c. onion chopped rinsed
1/2 lb of sliced mushrooms
10 oz. pkg of frozen corn
1 14.5 oz. can of diced tomatoes
1 c. low fat shredded cheddar
or 2 c. fresh tomatoes cheese
8 oz. tomato sauce

Heat olive oil and garlic in large pan. Add onions, green pepper, and mushrooms. Cook until tender. Add in tomato sauce, diced tomatoes, chili powder, and bring to boil. Turn down to low, add in zucchini and kidney beans. Simmer for 10-15 minutes. Add frozen corn and 1/2 cup cheddar cheese. Stir. Simmer on low for additional 10-15 minutes. Serve topped with cheddar cheese.

Note: Calories: 195 Total Fat: 3g Protein: 13g Total Carbohydrates: 34g Dietary Fiber: 9g Sugars: 6g

CHICKEN CASSEROLE

1 cup cubed, cooked skinless chicken breast
4 oz. can mushrooms
3/4 c. water
3 cups Schwan®'s Summer Garden Pasta Blend (shells, carrots, peas, green beans)
salt substitute
pepper to taste
garlic powder to taste
10 3/4oz 98% fat-free cream of chicken soup
onion powder to taste
1 c. fat-free shredded cheddar cheese

Preheat oven to 350 degrees. Cook pasta blend as directed. Mix soup, water and remaining ingredients (reserve 1/2 cup cheese to sprinkle on top) Add salt/pepper/garlic powder/onion powder to taste. Bake in casserole dish sprayed with non-stick spray at 350 degrees until bubbly, about 25-30 minutes

Note: Calories: 346Fat: 6 grams Protein: 21 grams Carbohydrate: 52 grams Cholesterol: 55 mg Sodium: 1457 mg Sugar: 2.5 grams

CHICKEN DIVAN

2 chicken breasts, boneless 2 T. grapeseed or olive oil
skinless, cut into bite size I can cream of chicken soup
pieces 1/2 c. mayonnaise
1 1/2lb chopped broccoli 1 tsp. lemon juice
1 T. minced garlic 2 c. cheddar cheese
Place broccoli in the bottom of 9x13 baking dish. Heat oil in skillet and
add garlic, sauté for a few minutes and then add chicken. Cook
chicken
until cooked through. Place chicken on top of broccoli. Mix the soup,
lemon juice and mayonnaise and pour over top of chicken. Top with
cheese and bake at 350 degrees for 40 minutes. Goes great with rice!

CHICKEN ROLLANTINI WITH SPINACH

8 chicken cutlets (pounded thin)
6 T. part skim ricotta cheese
1/2 c. whole wheat Italian seasoned breadcrumbs
6 oz. part skim mozzarella, shredded
1/4 c. grated Parmesan cheese
Non-stick cooking spray
6 T. egg whites
1 c. marinara sauce
5 oz. frozen spinach, squeezed dry of any liquid
Wash and dry chicken cutlets and season with salt & pepper Preheat
oven to 450° Spray baking dish with non-stick cooking spray. Combine
breadcrumbs with 2 tablespoons grated parmesan cheese and place
in a bowl. Place 1/4 cup egg whites in another bowl. Combine 1.5 oz
mozzarella cheese with remaining grated parmesan cheese, spinach,
2 tbsp egg whites, and ricotta cheese. Lay thin chicken cutlets on
working surface and spread 2 tbsp of spinach-cheese mixtures on
each. Loosely roll each one and keep seam side down. Dip chicken in
egg mixture then in breadcrumb mixture, and place seam side down in
baking dish. Repeat with remaining chicken. Lightly spray chicken
rollantinis with non-stick spray Bake 25 minutes in oven. Remove, top
with sauce and then remaining shredded mozzarella cheese. Bake 3
more minutes, until cheese is melted and bubbling. Serve with
additional sauce on side and grated parmesan cheese.
Note: 1 serving (~1 stuffed breast) Total calories: 268 Total fat: 9 g
Total carbohydrates: 8 g Protein: 36 g

CHINESE BONELESS RIBS
I tsp. canola oil
I T. five spice powder
2 lbs boneless pork ribs
I T. black vinegar
2 cloves minced garlic
1/4 c. soy sauce
I T. red pepper flakes
2 T. lime juice
I sm. onion, minced
I tsp. sesame oil
Heat the oil in a large skillet. Cook the pork for I minute on each side. Place in a slow cooker. Pour the remaining ingredients over the meat. Cover and cook on low for 8 hours. If the sauce is very thin, pour into a saucepan and cook until it reduces. Drizzle the sauce on the ribs and serve.
Note: Calories: 530 | Fat: 26g | Carbs: 7g | Protein: 64g

CLASSIC CUBAN SANDWICHES
I loaf of Cuban bread
1/2 lb. Swiss cheese, sliced
I lb. cooked ham, sliced
yellow mustard
I lb. roasted pork, sliced
Dill pickle slices
Preheat grill to medium heat (about 375°); coat with nonstick cooking spray. Cut bread into quarters; slice each quarter lengthwise. Spread with mustard; layer on pickles, ham, pork and cheese. Place sandwich on hot grate. Press sandwiches to 1/3 of original height by putting a clean, heavy skillet on top. Leave the skillet on sandwich; continue grilling for two minutes. Turn sandwich over and repeat. Slice each sandwich in half.
Note: Makes 4 sandwiches.

CROCK POT TORTILLA SOUP

Holly Keating
1 box of chicken broth
1 pkt of MSG free taco
1 box of beef broth seasoning
3 breast of chicken cut up, sliced
1 can of black beans
1 can of corn
fresh Cilantro to taste
1 pkt of star noodles (found in Pickled Jalapeño ethnic aisle)

Noodles are cooked in broth set aside and add at the end. Garnish with shredded cheddar cheese(Borden's melts best) And crush tortilla chips or home made.

FRENCH DIP SANDWICHES

1 can beer (optional)
3 buds garlic, minced
10 beef bouillon cubes
1 T. sugar
salt and pepper
Tops of celery
1 tsp. oregano
1 1/2 lg onions
3 bay leaves
5 lb boneless beef rump roast

Put all ingredients into at least a 6 - qt. kettle, on top of beef rump roast. Cover with water and bring to a boil. Boil gently for 3 hours. Remove, and cool roast in refrigerator, then slice thinly. Chill broth; skim and strain. Marinate beef slices in juice for 24 hours in refrigerator. Serve beef on hard rolls with side dish of hot juice to dip.

GARLICKY CHICKEN AND VEGETABLE SAUTÉ

4 boneless, skinless chicken breasts (about 2lbs)
I c. canned chicken broth with roasted garlic
I tsp. dry Montreal chicken
I pkg. (10 oz) frozen pepper and seasoning onion stir-fry
mixture, thawed, patted dry
2 T. olive oil
I can sliced new potatoes, drained and patted dry
I T. drained capers
I T. chopped fresh parsley
2 tsp. cornstarch

Sprinkle chicken with seasoning. In large nonstick skillet, heat I T. oil over high heat. Add chicken; cook, turning once, until golden, about 4 minutes each side. Transfer chicken to platter; reserve. To same skillet, add remaining oil; heat over medium heat. Add potatoes; cook, turning once until golden, 3 minutes each side. Transfer to platter with chicken; reserve. Whisk cornstarch into chicken broth. Add broth mixture to skillet; over high heat, heat to a boil. Add pepper mixture, then reserved chicken and potatoes; sprinkle with capers and parsley. Reduce heat to low; cover and cook until meat thermometer inserted into chicken registers 165°F, 10-15 minutes. Transfer to platter and serve.

Note: Servings: 4; Calories: 377; Fat: 13g; Carbs: 12g; Protein: 50g

HAMBURGER AND CABBAGE

Carla Harrison
I 1/2 lbs lean ground beef
I sweet, red pepper
I lrg. head cabbage
I clove garlic, minced
I onion
salt and pepper to taste

Brown onion, garlic and hamburger together in a large skillet or Dutch oven. Chop cabbage and pepper and add to cooked hamburger. Add 1/2 cup of water and cover with lid. Cook until cabbage and pepper are done, approximately 15 to 20 minutes. Season to taste and enjoy.

HEALTHY CHICKEN VEGETABLE CASSEROLE

12 oz cooked chicken breasts, diced
7 oz penne pasta, whole wheat
2 yellow or orange bell peppers, chopped
2 T. all purpose flour
2 T. butter, unsalted
1 zucchini, chopped
10 oz skim milk
2 heads broccoli, approx. 12 oz, chopped
1 pinch white pepper
1 tsp Italian seasoning
1/3 c. Monterey jack cheese
1 T. Parmesan cheese
Nonstick cooking spray

Prepare the white sauce by placing the butter in a small sauce pot that has been preheated over medium heat. Once the butter foams, add flour and stir for 1 minute; try not to let the mixture turn brown. Add milk to the mixture and continue to stir until it starts to bubble. Reduce heat and simmer for 10 minutes. Add pepper, Italian seasoning and Parmesan cheese to the sauce. Stir to combine. Cook pasta according to package directions. While pasta is cooking, preheat oven to 350 degrees. During the last minute of the pasta's cooking, add the chopped broccoli to the water. Allow to simmer for one minute. Drain the pasta and broccoli. Spritz the bottom and sides of a 9 X 13 oven-proof casserole dish with nonstick cooking spray. In a large bowl, combine the pasta and broccoli with the chicken and chopped vegetables; cover with the sauce. Place in the baking dish. Sprinkle with the Monterey jack cheese and cover with foil. Bake for 20 minutes; remove foil and continue to bake until cheese is melted.

Note: Calories: 320.6 Total Fat: 8.9 g Carbs: 36.1 g Protein: 27.9 g

ITALIAN CLAMS
24 Pacific Littleneck (or any hard-shell) clams
2 T. parsley, finely chopped
2 c. Italian bread crumbs
2 garlic cloves, finely minced
2 T. extra virgin olive oil
1/4 c. fresh oregano, minced

Preheat grill to high heat (about 450°); coat with nonstick cooking spray. Wash clams very thoroughly and place on grate. In saucepan, combine garlic, oregano, parsley, breadcrumbs, and oil; mix well and heat. Clam shells will open after about 5 to 6 minutes. Discard any clams that haven't opened. using oven mitts, lift top shell, scoop a spoonful of seasoned breading mixture in each and heat additional minute or two. Serve immediately.
Note: Makes 4 six piece servings.

LEMON PEPPER SALMON
I large salmon fillet
1/8 c. lemon juice
1/8 c. lemon pepper seasoning (or more to taste)

Pre-heat oven to 350°. On a baking sheet, place a piece of aluminum foil, 2 times the size of the salmon fillet, Place the salmon fillet in the center of the foil. Pour lemon juice on salmon fillet. Sprinkle the lemon pepper seasoning on the salmon fillet. Bake for 30-40 minutes or until salmon is flaky.

LOADED CAULIFLOWER CASSEROLE

Carla Harrison
2 lbs cauliflower florets
4 T. heavy cream
8 oz shredded sharp cheddar cheese, divided
2 bunches green onions, sliced (1 1/2 c.)
8 oz shredded Monterrey jack cheese, divided
6 slices bacon, cooked and crumbled
8 oz block cream cheese, softened
1 clove garlic, grated
salt and pepper to taste

Preheat oven to 350°. Steam cauliflower florets until tender. While cauliflower steams, cream together 6 oz of the shredded cheddar, 6 oz of the Monterrey Jack, cream cheese, and heavy cream. Stir in sliced green onions, chopped bacon, and garlic. Set aside. Drain any liquid from steamed cauliflower and add to cheese mixture. Stir cauliflower and
cheese mixture together. Taste for seasoning, and add as necessary. If you want a finer texture, give a few mashes with the potato masher. Pour into a 2-3 quart casserole and sprinkle on remaining cheddar and Monterrey Jack cheese. Cover dish with foil and bake for 25 minutes; remove foil and continue to bake until cheese is brown and bubbly.
Note: Can be mashed for the mushy phase as well.

LOW CARB VEGGIE PIZZA

2 low carb tortilla wraps (large)
3/4 c. diced tomatoes
1/2 c. reduced fat chive and onion cream cheese
1/8c. diced green pepper
1/8c.diced cucumbers
1/2 c. light sour cream
3/4 c. light shredded Colby and Monterey jack cheese
1 pkg dry ranch dressing mix
1/8c. shredded carrots
1/2 c. sliced black olives
3/4 c. raw broccoli

Mix cream cheese, sour cream, and dressing packet together and spread evenly on tortillas. Top with veggies and olives and sprinkle with cheese. Cut each tortilla into 4 pieces and serve
Note: Calories: 170Fat: 10 grams Protein: 10 grams Carbohydrate: 12 g

MEAT AND BEANS
I lb hamburger, cooked and crumbly
2 lrg. cans baked beans
1/4 c. brown sugar
I lb bacon, cooked crisp and crumbled
I lb. fully cooked smoked sausage, sliced
In large slow cooker add all ingredients and cook on low for 4-6 hours. Stirring occasionally. Serve as a meal or as a side dish.

MEATLOAF BITES
Jennifer at 7 Bites
I lb. lean ground chuck
I egg, beaten
Parmesan cheese (optional)
Glaze:
dash of steak sauce, approx 2 T.
dash of Ketchup, about a 1/2 cup
Pre-heat oven to 425°. Make glaze. add half of glaze to meat and egg mixture. do not over mix it. Do not over mix. Use an ice cream scooper to scoop meat mixture into mini muffin pan. put some of the glaze on top of the meat mixture. Bake for 15 minutes or until meat temperature reaches 155 - 165°.

MEXICAN CHICKEN AND RICE
I can fat free cream of mushroom soup
11/2 c. instant rice
I pkg taco seasoning
I can fat free cream of chicken soup
cilantro and green onions, chopped (optional)
2 cans water
3 lbs frozen boneless, skinless chicken breasts (6 breasts)
I can black beans, drained and rinsed
I c. shredded cheddar cheese
I can Rotel® diced tomatoes with chilies
Preheat the oven to 350.Coat a 13x9 inch glass casserole dish with cooking spray. In a medium bowl, whisk together the soups, water and taco seasoning, then pour into the bottom of the dish. Sprinkle the rice over the soups, then place the chicken breasts (still frozen) on top. Pour the beans and tomatoes over the chicken, then sprinkle on the cilantro and green onions. Cover with foil and bake for 1 hour, 40 minutes. Remove foil, sprinkle shredded cheese over to melt and bake another 10 minutes.
Note: Calories: 268.9 | Fat: 4.9g | Protein: 34.6g | Carbs: 19.3g

MEXICAN CHICKEN STUFFED SHELLS

Tammy McCoy

4 c. boneless, skinless chicken breasts, cooked and diced with chiles (don't drain)
2 cans petite diced tomatoes
I can black beans, drained and rinsed
1/4 to 1/2 c. chicken stock
I tsp cumin
6 green onions, diced
1 1/2 c. sharp cheddar cheese, shredded
1/2 each of red, green, yellow, orange bell peppers (or 2 whole bell peppers of your choice), diced
I c. picante sauce
38 large pasta shells, cooked al dente
3 (8oz) blocks cream cheese, softened

Cook pasta shells in well salted, boiling water until al dente (still have a little bite to them) If you cook them too long, they will be difficult to stuff, plus they will have additional cooking time, once they are stuffed. Drain the pasta and set aside while you make the filling. Cook, drain and dice enough chicken breast to make 4 cups. You could use canned chicken broth if you prefer. To make the filling, mix diced chicken, drained black beans, green onions, diced peppers, and cumin in a large mixing bowl. Thoroughly incorporate all the ingredients. In a separate bowl, mix the cream cheese, chicken stock and undrained tomatoes with chiles. When thoroughly combined, pour it over the chicken mixture and mix well. (If you have trouble incorporating the cream cheese and tomatoes, you can heat it slightly in the microwave.) Spread 3/4c. picante sauce in the bottom of a large baking pan (2 - 13x9 pans). Reserve the final 1/4 cup, for later. Using a spoon, or your fingers, fill each of your cooked and cooled pasta shells, setting them into the picante covered pan. Continue until all shells are filled and arranged in the pan. When the pan is full, drizzle the shells with the remaining 1/4 cup of picante and then sprinkle with the shredded cheddar cheese. Cover the baking pan tightly with foil and bake at 350 degrees for about 30 minutes or until hot and bubbly.

MEXICAN LASAGNA
Dianna Gill
I lb ground beef, browned, drained and rinsed
I can low-fat refried beans
shredded lettuce (optional)
I pkt taco seasoning
sour cream for dipping
I can peeled/diced tomatoes (or can use fresh)
I pkg cream cheese, softened
non-stick cooking spray
6-8 flour tortillas
I c. water
I c. salsa
I sm. can diced black olives (optional)
I (16oz) pkg shredded Colby cheese, divided

Add water and taco seasoning to cooked ground beef. Simmer 20 minutes or until liquid is gone. Preheat oven to 350°. Spray square glass casserole baking dish with cooking spray. Place 2-3 tortillas in the bottom of the dish. Add refried beans, cream cheese, beef mixture, salsa, 1/2 of the shredded cheese. Add 2-3 tortillas on top of that and then add remaining beef mixture and cheese. Bake for 20-30 minutes or until cheese is melted. Add diced tomatoes and lettuce and serve with sour cream. Enjoy.

Note: To use this recipe during the mushy stage, simply exclude the tortillas and purée the mixture after cooking.

MOM'S BEEF STEW
Jennifer and Sue at 7 Bites
2 lbs stew meat dredged in 1/2 c. soy flour and seasoned with salt and pepper to taste
1/2 medium bag baby carrots
1/2 large onion, chopped
I clove garlic
2 T. oil
2 sprigs fresh rosemary
I box beef broth
2 T. road kill seasoning (garlic powder, salt and pepper)
2 T. tomato paste
2 medium red potatoes, cut into bite size pieces
I c. wine (red or white)

Stove top: Brown dredged and seasoned stew meat in oil in large stock pot. De-glaze pan using 1 c beef broth. Add tomato paste and mix well. Add remaining broth and wine and stir well to combine. Add remaining ingredients and stir. Bring to a boil over medium high heat then reduce heat to medium low. Simmer for up to 2 hours, stirring occasionally. Add more broth if it looks as though the liquid is evaporating too quickly. Slow Cooker: Brown dredged and seasoned stew meat in oil. De-glaze pan with 1 C beef broth. Transfer to slow cooker and add remaining ingredients. Stir well to combine. Cook on low for up to 12 hours or on high for up to 8 hours. If it looks like the liquid is evaporating too quickly after a couple of hours, add more broth. Variations: Add a handful of greens to the stew during the last 15-20 minutes for a great veggie boost! * Use whatever veggies you have on hand! Green beans, scallions, turnips, sweet potatoes ... any hardy vegetable works great!

Note: Nutrition per 1/2 C serving: Calories: 224 Carbs: 9g Protein: 17g

MONGOLIAN BEEF

3 lbs lean beef bottom roast, extra fat removed
1/2 c. low sodium soy sauce
2 T. black vinegar
3 cloves garlic, grated
2 T. hoisin sauce
1" knob peeled fresh ginger, grated
1 T. five spice powder
1 T. cornstarch
1 medium onion, thinly sliced
1 tsp. red pepper flakes
1/2 c. water
1 tsp. sesame oil

Place all ingredients into a slow cooker. Cover and cook on low for 5 hours or until the meat is thoroughly cooked through and tender. Remove the roast to a cutting board. Slice thinly and return to the slow cooker. Cook for an additional 20 minutes on high. Stir the meat and the sauce before serving.

Note: Calories: 490 | Fat: 27g | Carbs: 10g | Protein: 49g

PEPPERY CHICKEN WINGS

Joan S
16 chicken wings (2 lbs)
1/4 c. crumbled blue cheese (1 oz)
1 tsp. peanut or vegetable oil
1 tsp. cayenne pepper
1/2 small yellow onion, grated
1/2 cup plain low-fat yogurt
1 tsp. cider vinegar
1/4 c. buttermilk

Preheat broiler. Separate the chicken wings at the joint and remove the wing tips. In a medium size bowl, combine the peanut oil, cayenne pepper; add the chicken wings and turn until well coated. Place the wings on the broiler pan rack and broil about 8 inches from the heat, turning occasionally, until crisp and golden - about 20 minutes. Meanwhile, prepare the dip. In a medium-size bowl, whisk together the yogurt, buttermilk, blue cheese, onion and vinegar; transfer to a small serving dish. Set the dip in the center of a warm large round platter and arrange the broiled chicken wings around it. Serves 8.

PIZZA BURGERS

2 lb hamburger
1/4 c. Parmesan cheese
1/2 lb Mozzarella cheese
1 T. garlic salt
1 can tomato soup
1 T. oregano
1/4 btl. chili sauce salt and pepper

Brown hamburger, drain off grease and rinse thoroughly under hot water. Grate cheese. Mix all ingredients together. Fill buttered buns. Wrap individually in foil (for oven) or cling wrap (for microwave). **Note:** Yield: about 24 burgers. These freeze well. To reheat in oven, bake at 350° for 20 minutes or in microwave for about 3 minutes.

PULLED PORK

Carla Harrison

1 (8lb) whole picnic pork shoulder or pork shoulder butt
11/2 tsp. salt (or more to taste)
3 T. onion powder
3 T. brown sugar
1/2 c. Dijon mustard
1 c. water
11/2 T. black pepper
1 c. Low Carb BBQ sauce
11/2 T. garlic powder

With oven rack in lowest position, preheat to 250 degrees. Remove rind from pork roast. Mix together dry ingredients to make a rub. Place pork on a rack in shallow roasting pan. Rub the pork all over with Dijon mustard, then pat on dry rub. Roast covered pork until a meat thermometer reads 170 degrees. This can take anywhere from 9 to 11 hours. Remove pork from oven and let cool for about 1 hour. Reserve all pan drippings. Pull pork into chunks, and then shred into a large bowl. In medium saucepan, combine reserved drippings (skim off most of the fat), 1 cup water, and barbecue sauce. Simmer for 5 minutes, then pour over shredded pork. Stir well. This can now be refrigerated and reheated in a covered pot over low heat later, or served immediately.

Note: Low Carb BBQ Sauce recipe is in the section called This and That.

SLOPPY JOE SQUARES

Tammy McCoy

1 lb extra lean ground beef (or ground turkey)
2 c. shredded Cheddar cheese
1 T. sesame seeds
1 can (15.5oz) sloppy joe sauce
2 (12oz each) cans refrigerated
crescent dinner rolls

Preheat oven to 350°F. In 10-inch skillet, cook beef over medium heat 8 to 10 minutes, stirring occasionally, until thoroughly cooked; drain. Stir in sauce. Heat to boiling, stirring occasionally. Unroll 1 can of the dough; place in ungreased 13x9-inch (3-quart) glass baking dish. Press in bottom and 1/2 inch up sides of dish. Spread beef mixture over dough; sprinkle with cheese. Unroll second can of dough; place over cheese. Sprinkle with sesame seed. Bake 30 to 35 minutes or until mixture is bubbly and dough is golden brown. Cut into squares to serve.

SLOW COOKER BEEF STEW
Carla Harrison
1 pkt Pioneer® homestyle meatloaf seasoning
1/4 c. vegetable oil
4 c. water
2 lbs of stewed beef meat
2 pkgs Pioneer® brown gravy mix (makes 4 cups)
2 lrg cans of homestyle VegAll
1/2 c. of flour

Coat the beef with flour. Put the vegetable oil in a pan and sear the coated beef just until brown. Put water and seasoning in crock pot and whisk together. Add seared beef and cans of VegAll. Cook on high setting for 6 hours. At end of time add the brown gravy mix and whisk it into the stew. Then serve.
Note: Makes 6-8 servings.

SLOW COOKER CHICKEN TACO FILLING
16 oz. (1 lb) skinless, boneless chicken breasts
1 (1.25 oz.) pkg dry taco seasoning
1 c. chicken broth

Mix chicken broth and taco seasoning in a bowl. Place chicken breast in slow cooker. Pour broth and seasoning mixture over chicken. Cover and cook on low for 6-8 hours. Shred chicken. Cook on low for additional 30 minutes to absorb excess juices. Serve as filling for tacos, topping for a salad or by itself for a protein source.
Note: Calories: 148 Total Fat: 2.4 g Carbs: 6 g Protein: 23 g

SLOW COOKER HONEY WINGS
3 lbs chicken wings, tips removed
1/2 tsp. ground black pepper
2 T. chili sauce
1/4 c. honey
1/2 tsp garlic powder
1/4 c. low sodium soy sauce

Place the wings in a slow cooker. In a small bowl, mix the honey, soy sauce, pepper, chili sauce and garlic. Pour over the wings. Toss to coat with sauce. Cook for 6-7 hours on low. Stir before serving.
Note: Calories: 340 | Fat: 22g | Carbs: 8g | Protein: 25g

SLOW COOKER ORANGE CHICKEN
2 lrg carrots, peeled and sliced about 1/2 - inch thick
1 tsp. salt
1/2 tsp. pepper
2 lrg red or green bell peppers, cut into 1/2 inch chunks
8 oz orange juice concentrate
2 c. Mandarin orange segments or fresh orange segments
3 cloves garlic, finely minced
4 boneless skinless chicken
2 green onions, chopped
hot cooked rice
2 tsp. ground ginger

Put carrots, peppers, garlic, then the chicken, ginger, salt, pepper & frozen orange juice in Crockpot. Cover and cook on LOW 4 to 6 hours. Serve chicken on hot cooked rice on platter. Top with orange segments and green onions. Serve chicken liquid in gravy boat, if desired.

SLOW COOKER SWEET GARLIC CHICKEN
4-6 chicken breasts, boneless, skinless
2-3 T. minced garlic
1 tsp. fresh ground pepper
1 c. packed brown sugar
2 T. corn starch
2/3 c. vinegar (apple cider or white)
2 T. water
red pepper flakes (optional)
1/4 c. lemon-lime soda (diet or regular)

Spray slow cooker with non-stick cooking spray. Place chicken (frozen, thawed or fresh) inside slow cooker. Mix together brown sugar, vinegar, soda, garlic, soy sauce, and pepper together. Pour over chicken. Cook on low for 6-8 hours or high for 4 hours. Take chicken pieces out of slow cooker and pour remaining sauce into saucepan. Place saucepan over high heat. Mix together corn starch and water, pour into saucepan, and mix well. Let sauce come to a boil and boil for 2-3 minutes, or until it starts to thicken and turns into a glaze. Remove from heat and let sit for a minute or two (it will continue to thicken as it cools down). Sprinkle red pepper flakes on top if desired

SLOW COOKER TERIYAKI STEAK
Carla Harrison
I lb boneless chuck steak
2 T. oil
1/2 c. soy sauce
I T. Splenda®
I tsp ground ginger
I clove garlic, minced
Cut steak into ⅛" thick slices. Combine remaining ingredients in bowl. Place meat in slow cooker, pour over sauce and stir. Cover and cook low heat 8 hours.

SLOW COOKER THREE BEAN CHILI
I tsp. fresh jalapeño, minced
2 tsp jalapeño hot sauce (optional)
30 oz canned tomato, diced
2 stalks celery, diced
15 oz can of black beans, drained and rinsed
I medium onion, diced
3 cloves garlic, minced
15 oz can of kidney beans, drained and rinsed
2 carrots, diced
I tsp ground cayenne
15 oz can of cannellini beans, drained and rinsed
I tsp chili powder
I tsp paprika
I cup fresh corn kernels
I tsp cumin
Place all ingredients except corn into a slow cooker. Cook for 8 hours on low. Add corn and stir. Cover and continue cooking for 1/2 hour on low. Stir before serving.
Note: Calories: 180 | Fat: 1.5g | Carbs: 39g | Protein: 9g

SPICY CHICKEN SPAGHETTI

Tammy McCoy

1 (8 oz) pkg spaghetti
4 cooked chicken breast halves, chopped
Non-stick cooking spray
1/4 c. margarine
1 (10oz) can cream of chicken soup
1/2 c. large onion, chopped
1 (8oz) Velveeta® cheese, cubed
1 (10oz.) can tomatoes & chiles (Rotel)

Preheat oven to 350° degrees. Cook spaghetti according to directions, drain. Place in 13x9 baking dish coated with cooking spray. Melt margarine in large skillet over medium heat. Add onion and sauté 3-5 minutes until tender. Add cheese and tomatoes and chiles, stirring until cheese melts. Stir in chicken and soup, blending well. Pour mixture over spaghetti in baking dish. Bake at 350° degree for 25 minutes or until bubbly. Tip: Split the spaghetti and mixture into two separate pans for easier cooking.

SUSAN'S AMAZING MEATLOAF

Susan Jean Holub

1 lb extra lean ground beef
2 egg whites
1 1/2 slices multi-grain or whole wheat bread or 1 c. bread crumbs
1/3 c. steak sauce, divided
2 T. Worcestershire sauce
1/2 tsp. garlic powder
1 c. onions, diced
1/2 tsp. salt
3/4 c. red bell pepper, diced
black pepper to taste

Preheat oven to 350 degrees. Line a baking sheet with foil. Coat with cooking spray. To make bread crumbs: toast bread. Break into pieces and place in blender. Pulse into crumbs. In a large bowl, add ground beef, bread crumbs, onions, red bell pepper, egg whites, 3 tablespoons steak sauce, Worcestershire sauce, garlic powder, salt and pepper. Using your hands, mix together all the ingredients. Place meat mixture on baking sheet and free form a loaf by hand. It should be about 12"x4." Using the back of a spoon or knife, spread the top of loaf with remaining 2 tablespoons of steak sauce. Bake in oven for 1 hour. Allow to stand 5 minutes before cutting into 12 slices. Makes 12 slices, each serving 2 slices.

Note: 162 calories, 4 grams of fat

TACO BAKE

Tammy McCoy
1 lb extra lean ground beef, browned, drained and rinsed
1/2 c. Salsa Con Queso
1 1/2 - 2 c. shredded mexican cheese blend
1 pkt taco seasoning
3/4 c. water
3 large flour tortillas (8-inch size)
Add in taco seasoning and water to beef in a skillet, simmer for 20 minutes, uncovered or until liquid is absorbed. Once the taco meat is ready, turn off heat and add in 1/2 cup salsa con queso. Give it a good stir until thoroughly combined. Preheat oven to 350° degrees. Spray an 8-inch round baking pan with nonstick cooking spray. Layer the bottom of the pan with a flour tortilla. Add about ⅓ of the ground beef taco filling on the first layer. Then add ⅓ of the shredded cheese. Continue until you are done with all the layers: another tortilla, more taco mixture, more cheese. Bake at 350° degrees for about 15-20 minutes. Until cheese is melted and edges are slightly golden brown. Allow to cool for a couple of minutes. Then slice and serve.

TACO GRANDE

Tammy McCoy

8 (6-7 inch) flour tortillas, divided
2 c. shredded Colby & Monterey jack cheese blend, divided
I lb lean ground turkey
I green onion, chopped finely
2 T. taco seasoning mix
4 c. shredded lettuce
1/2 c. water
1/2 c. low fat or fat free sour cream
I jar (16 oz) salsa, divided

Preheat oven to 350°F. Spray bottom and sides of Deep Dish Baker
with nonstick cooking spray. Arrange four tortillas in bottom of baker,
overlapping slightly. In large (12-in.) skillet, cook ground turkey over
medium heat 8-10 minutes or until no longer pink, breaking turkey
into small crumbles. Drain, if necessary. Add taco seasoning mix and
water; cook according to package directions. Remove from heat; stir
in I cup of the salsa. Spoon turkey mixture evenly over tortillas in
baker. Sprinkle with I cup of the cheese. Sprinkle half of the green
onion over cheese. Top with remaining four tortillas, overlapping
slightly and pressing down lightly. Spread remaining salsa over tortillas.
Sprinkle with remaining cheese and onion. Bake 28-30 minutes or until
cheese is melted. Remove from oven; let stand 5 minutes. Cut into
wedges. Serve with lettuce and sour cream.

Note: Makes 8 servings. Calories 420, Fat 19 g, Carbs 39 g, Protein
23 g,

TACO PIE

Tammy McCoy
1/4 c. butter
1/2 c. salsa
2/3c. milk
1 c. shredded lettuce
1 pkg taco seasoning mix
1 medium tomato, chopped
2 1/2 c. mashed potato flakes (or left over mashed potatoes)
1 c. sharp cheddar cheese, shredded
1 lb lean ground beef sour cream (optional)
1/2 c. chopped onion

Preheat oven to 350° degrees. In a medium sauce pan, melt butter. Add milk and 2 tablespoon taco seasoning. Remove from heat and add potato flakes until incorporated. Press mixture into the bottom of a 10- inch pan. Bake for 7-10 minutes until it just BARELY turns golden brown. In a medium skillet, cook beef and onions until beef is browned and cooked through. Drain. Add Salsa and remaining taco seasoning. Cook until bubbly. Pour into crust. Bake for 15 minutes, or until crust is golden brown. Let cool for 5 minutes. Top with cheese, lettuce, and tomatoes. Cut and serve with sour cream.

Note: If using left-over mashed potatoes, omit the butter and milk. Also, if puréed this recipe can work for the mushy phase as well.

TATER TOT CASSEROLE

Tammy McCoy
2 lbs. extra lean ground beef
1 c. grated low-fat cheddar cheese (or more to taste)
1 can cream of mushroom soup
1 (16oz) container low-fat or fat free Sour Cream
1 pkg frozen tater tots

Preheat oven to 350° degrees. Grease or spray non-stick cooking spray in a 13x9 inch pan. Layer the beef on the bottom of the pan, set aside. In a med mixing bowl add sour cream and mushroom soup and mix well. Then layer the mixture on top of the beef, then add cheese. Top with tater tots. Bake covered for 45 minutes. Uncover and bake 15 minutes longer, adding extra cheese here if desired.

Note: This recipe doubles as a mushy phase recipe, if you exclude the tater tots.

THREE CHEESE CHICKEN ALFREDO BAKE

Dianna Gill

1 (16oz) box Penne pasta noodles
2-3 c. cooked, shredded or diced chicken
1 (10oz) container Alfredo sauce
1 c. Parmesan cheese
1 c. low fat sour cream
1 (8oz) bag Mozzarella cheese
1 c. low fat Ricotta cheese

Pre-make chicken in crock pot. When chicken is done: Boil penne pasta in a large pot of water, according to package directions. Drain water and place noodles & shredded chicken in 9 X13 glass baking dish. Mix together in large bowl; Alfredo sauce, sour cream and ricotta & layer evenly over the noodles & chicken. Top with Parmesan cheese & mozzarella. Cover with foil & bake at 350° for 30 minutes, or until hot and bubbly.

TOMATO PIE

Kacie VanderZon

3 good-sized tomatoes
1 c. basil, thinly chopped
Sea salt
2 c. mozzarella cheese, shredded
Freshly ground pepper
Pillsbury pie crust
1/4 c. extra light olive oil

Thinly slice your tomatoes in rounds and others in half-rounds and lay them out on a few layers of paper towel to dry. Season them with sea salt and pepper and let them sit for 20-30 minutes. Spread the pie crust in a shallow pan of any shape and bake the crust for 10-15 minutes at 300-325°F so the bottom gets a little brown. Let cool. Place a thin layer of chopped basil to the baked crust. Add shredded mozzarella cheese. Arrange the tomatoes to fill the pan and drizzle 1/4 c. or less of extra light olive oil on top. Bake at 325°F for 20-30 minutes. The cheese should be bubbling up through the tomatoes. Let it sit for 30 minutes before you serve. Slice, then pop it back in the oven for a few minutes to warm.

TROPICAL CHICKEN SALAD
2 c. cubed, cooked chicken
2 large, firm bananas, sliced
I c. celery, finely chopped
I (11oz) can mandarin oranges,
I c. low-fat mayonnaise drained
1/2 to I tsp curry powder (optional)
salad greens (optional)
3/4 c. salted peanuts or cashew(optional)
I 20oz can crushed pineapple halves (can use chunked)
Put chicken and celery in a large bowl. Add mayonnaise and curry
powder and mix into chicken mixture. Refrigerate until ready to serve
then add fruits and toss gently. Serve on salad greens and top with
nuts.
Note: This recipe can be made for mushy stage by puréeing or by
finely smashing the ingredients together. Omit the nuts and other large
food items to make it mushy phase.

TUNA SALAD
5 oz. canned Tuna in water, drained
2 T. Light or fat free Mayonnaise
2 T. relish
1/2 onion, diced
I large hard boiled egg, finely chopped
1/2 c. cheese
Blend all ingredients in a medium sized bowl. Add salt and pepper to
taste. Makes approximately 3 servings.
Note: Calories: 194.0 Fat: 7.8 g Carbs: 9.9 g Protein: 18.8 g

TURKEY MEATLOAF
2 lbs ground turkey, extra lean
I lrg egg
I pkg Stove Top® stuffing mix, herb blend
1/2 c. water
1/4 c. ketchup
Preheat oven to 350 degrees. Mix all the ingredients, but omit 1/8c.
Ketchup. Form into a loaf and place in a glass baking dish (make sure
there is enough room around edges). Glaze top with remaining
ketchup. Bake 350 degrees for 45-55 minutes. Inside should be 165+
degrees before serving. Number of Servings: 8
Note: Can be used during the mushy phase with the doctors
approval.
CALORIES: 220.6 | FAT: 2.7 g | PROTEIN: 28.5 g | CARBS: 13.3 g

VEGAN CHILI

4 cans tomato sauce
2 T. chili powder
I can pinto beans
I T. black pepper
I Vidalia onion, cubed
1/2 tsp cinnamon
I pkg Boca meatless ground crumbles
1/2 tsp nutmeg
I sm. square of Giradelli® 72% cocoa chocolate

In a non stick pan sauté the Boca Crumbles and the diced onion until onion in soft. Combine all ingredients in a slow cooker and cook on high for 3 hours, then switch to low until ready to eat. Makes 10 one cup servings

Note: CALORIES: 348.2 | FAT: 3 g | PROTEIN: 56.9 g | CARBS: 44.7 g | FIBER: 18.6 g

VEGETABLE, HAM AND CHEESE BAKE

I 1/2 c. cooked rotini (or any) pasta
I 1/2 c. cooked ham, diced
1/4 c. onion, diced
16oz pkg frozen broccoli, cauliflower, carrots, squash, zucchini blend, thawed
I garlic clove, minced
1/2 c. buttery crackers, crushed
(optional)
1/2 c. fat-free sour cream
1/4 tsp ground pepper
1/2 c. skim milk salt to taste
I 1/2 c. low-fat shredded cheddar
cheese, divided

Spray a 2 quart baking dish with non-stick cooking spray. Pre-heat oven to 350°. In a large bowl, mix sour cream, milk, one cup of cheese, ham, onion, garlic, and pepper; mix in the pasta and vegetables. Transfer to baking dish. Bake, uncovered, for 30 minutes. Add crackers and remaining cheese and cook an additional 10 minutes or until cheese is melted and bubbly.

Note: This can be puréed and used during the mushy phase if you leave out the crackers and pasta.

ZUCCHINI LASAGNA
2 1/2 T. extra virgin olive oil
3 T. oregano, fresh or dried
1 sm. onion, chopped
2 medium zucchini
1/2 tsp red pepper flakes
1 c. part-skim ricotta cheese (optional)
1/4 tsp. black pepper
1 lb. ground turkey
1/2 c. grated Parmesan cheese
1 28oz can petite diced tomatoes
salt to taste

Preheat oven to 375°. In medium skillet, add oil, onion and red pepper flakes and sauté for approximately 7-8 minutes. Add turkey and cook until brown. Add tomatoes and bring to a boil. Reduce heat and simmer until thickened for about 20 minutes. Stir in oregano, salt and pepper. Let cool. Meanwhile, slice the zucchini long wise into 1/8 inch thick strips. Put 5 or 6 slices, overlapping slightly, in bottom of an 8x8 - inch baking dish. Top with 1 cup of sauce. Dot with 1/4 c. ricotta cheese. Repeat layers twice, alternating the direction of the zucchini. Top with remaining zucchini and brush with oil. Dot with rest of ricotta. Top with Parmesan. Bake 50-60 minutes, until lasagna is bubbling and top is brown. Let stand for 10 minutes before serving. Serves 8.

Note: Purée a piece of this lasagna to enjoy during mushy phase.

6 BREADS AND ROLLS

Mushy Phase

ICE CREAM BREAD

Tammy McCoy
2 c. ice cream, any flavor
1 1/2 c. self-rising flour
Stir together ice cream and flour, stirring just until flour is moistened. Spoon batter into a greased and floured 8x4 inch loaf pan. Bake at 350° degrees for 40 to 45 minutes or until a wooden toothpick inserted in the center of the bread comes out clean. Remove from the pan, and cool on a wire rack.
Note: Add a scoop of your favorite protein powder to get your protein in for the day!

Solid Phase

APPLE-RAISIN MUFFINS

2 c. all purpose flour
1/4 c. butter, melted, cooled
3/4 c. packed light brown sugar
2 egg whites
2 tsp. baking powder
1 apple, preferably Gala or Fuji, peeled, cored, cut into 1/2"
pieces
1 tsp. ground cinnamon
1/2 tsp. salt
3/4 c. 1% milk
1/2 c. raisins

Preheat oven to 350°. Line 12 muffin cups with cupcake liners. In large bowl, mix flour, sugar, baking powder, cinnamon and salt. In separate bowl, stir together milk, butter and egg whites. Stir milk mixture into flour mixture until just blended. Stir in apple and raisins. Evenly divide batter between cupcake liners. Bake 20-25 minutes or until lightly browned and toothpick inserted into centers come out clean. Cool on cooling rack for 10 minutes. Serve warm.

Note: Calories: 200; Fat: 4g; Protein: 4g; Carbs: 38g

CARROT AND ZUCCHINI BREAD

2 c. flour 2 eggs
3/4 tsp. salt
1/4 c. olive oil
1/2 tsp. baking powder
1/4 c. applesauce
1/2 tsp. baking soda
3/4 c. brown sugar
1/2 tsp. cinnamon
1 c. grated zucchini
1/4 tsp. nutmeg
1 c. grated carrots

Preheat the oven to 375 degrees. Spray a 9 X 5 bread pan with cooking spray or cover with parchment paper. Combine the flour, salt, baking powder, baking soda, cinnamon, and nutmeg in a bowl.In another bowl combine the eggs, olive oil, and applesauce. Stir in the brown sugar. Then stir in the carrots and zucchini. Add the dry ingredients to the wet ingredients and stir until combined. Bake for 60-70 minutes until cooked through.

Note: 165 calories, 5.2g of fat, 26.8g of carbohydrates, 1g of fiber, 3.3g of protein

CREAM CHEESE PANCAKES

2 oz cream cheese
1/2 tsp cinnamon
2 eggs
1 packet Stevia® (or any) sweetener

Put all ingredients in a blender or magic bullet. Blend until smooth. Let rest for 2 minutes so the bubbles can settle. Pour 1/4 of the batter into a hot pan greased with butter or pam spray. Cook for 2 minutes until golden, flip and cook 1 minute on the other side. Repeat with the rest of the batter. Serve with sugar free syrup (or any syrup of your choice) and fresh berries.

Note: 344 calories, 29g fat, 2.5g net carbs, 17g protein

HIGH PROTEIN BREADSTICKS

1/3 pkg fast rising yeast
1/4 T parsley or 1/4 T caraway seeds or poppy seeds or coarse salt
1/4 tsp salt
3/8 c. soy flour
1/8 c. warm water
1/8 c. margarine (fat-free or 1/8c olive oil)

In a bowl, combine yeast, salt, and half of the flour. Stir in very warm water, beat vigorously. Stir in oil or butter. Put flour on slightly floured surface and knead until smooth and elastic. Mix in the rest of the flour to keep dough from sticking. Cover dough with plastic wrap and let it sit for 10 minutes. Preheat oven to 350 degrees F. Divide dough into 10 equal pieces. Shape each into a 10-12 inch rope. Sprinkle each rope with seasonings. Place ropes one inch apart on a cookie sheet and bake about 20 minutes or until golden and crisp.

Note: Fat 3g Carbohydrate 1g Protein 1g

HIGH PROTEIN PANCAKES
1/2 c. all-purpose flour
1 tsp cinnamon
2 tsp whole wheat flour
1 dash nutmeg
1/2 c. protein powder, unflavored
1 1/2 c. soy milk
1/4 c. Splenda® granular
1 tsp butter
1 tsp baking powder
2 eggs

Combine dry ingredients in medium bowl. Separately whisk milk, butter and eggs. Stir into dry until just moistened. In a nonstick skillet lightly sprayed with cooking spray, pour batter into 4 inches pancakes until all used.

Note: Total Fat 9g | Carbohydrate 22g | Protein 17g

MOIST BANANA BREAD
Tammy McCoy
3 or 4 ripe bananas, smashed
1 tsp. vanilla
⅓ c. melted butter
1 tsp baking soda
3/4 c. sugar pinch of salt
1 egg, beaten
1 1/2 c. all purpose flour

Preheat the oven to 350°F (175°C). With a spoon, mix butter with the smashed bananas in a large mixing bowl. Add in the sugar, egg, and vanilla. Next add in the baking soda and salt and mix in. Add the flour last, mix. Pour mixture into a buttered 4x8 inch loaf pan. Bake for 1 hour. Cool on a rack. Remove from pan and slice to serve.

MUFFIN IN A MINUTE

Carla Harrison
1/4 c. flax meal (or almond meal)
1 large egg
1/2 tsp. baking powder
1 tsp butter (or oil, yogurt, cream cheese, peanut butter, pumpkin, etc.)
1 pkt Splenda® (or sugar free syrup)
1 tsp. cinnamon (or cocoa, allspice, protein powder, fruit, etc.)

Put the ingredients in a coffee mug. Mix well. Microwave 1 minute (or more if you alter the recipe much). The shape of this can be changed by making it in a bowl or bread shaped plate. It can be "toasted" once it's cooked. Add water to make pancakes or crepes.

ROASTED VEGETABLE PANINI

3/4 c. roasted veggies Mustard
1/2 c. spinach Chipotle spread
1 100 calorie wrap or flatbread balsamic vinegar
1 oz (4 T.) part skim shredded cheese

Spread one half or whole flatbread with your chosen condiment. I love using this Chipotle spread, but any condiment or light dressing will work. Layer the spinach, roasted vegetables, and cheese on one half of the flatbread. Place a little cheese on both sides to help the sandwich stay together. Coat a pan with cooking spray and heat it over medium heat. Cook the sandwich on each side for 3-4 minutes or until toasted.
Note: 197 calories, 7.9g of fat, 21.9g of carbohydrates, 11.1g of fiber, 17.4g of protein, 1.2g of Sugar

7 DESSERTS

Liquid Phase

BANANA STRAWBERRY SHAKE

I ripe banana
1/4 c. egg substitute
3-4 large strawberries
I c. low-fat or fat free milk
I tsp. wheat germ

Add all ingredients into a blender and blend until smooth. Add ice if desired. Refrigerate any leftovers.

Note: Calories: 250 Fat: 2.5g Protein: 18g Carbs: 42g Fiber: 4g

Mushy Phase

BEST CHEESECAKE

2 c. low fat cottage cheese
1 lemon juice (rind if grated fresh)
2 eggs
1/2 c. low-fat sour cream
1 tsp vanilla extract
1/2 c. whey powder (vanilla)
1/4 c. Splenda® granular or other sugar substitute

Preheat oven to 375°F. Put the cottage cheese, eggs, sour cream, whey powder, Splenda, lemon rind an juice, and vanilla extract in a blender, and blend until very smooth. Pour mixed into a sprayed pie pan. Place the cake on the top rack of the oven and place a flat pan of water on the bottom rack. Bake for 30-40 minutes. Cook, then chill well before serving.

Note: Total Fat 3.5g | Carbohydrate 4g | Fiber 0g | Sugars 3g | Protein 9g

EGG CUSTARD

3 lrg eggs 2 c. milk
4 pkts artificial sweetener (Do NOT use Equal®)
1/4 tsp vanilla extract
1/8 tsp. grated nutmeg
1/4 tsp salt

Preheat oven to 350°. Beat the eggs in a large bowl. Stir in the artificial sweetener and salt, then the milk, vanilla, and nutmeg. Divide the mixture among six 4-ounce custard cups. Set the cups in a large baking dish and add enough hot water to fill the dish with 1 inch of water. Bake until set, about 30 minutes. Serve warm, room temperature, or chilled.

EGGNOG CUSTARD PIE

3 eggs
1/8 tsp salt
2 c. Lactaid® Eggnog (or any other eggnog)
1 tsp vanilla
1/4 tsp nutmeg
1/3 c. sugar (or granulated sugar substitute)
1/4 tsp cinnamon
1/4 tsp allspice
1/2 tsp. brandy or rum extract (optional)
1/4 tsp ground cloves (optional)
1 refrigerated pie crust

Preheat oven to 350°. Unroll pie crust and place in a 9 inch pie pan. Pack crust into pie plate leaving no air spaces between crust and pan. In a large bowl, beat eggs, sugar, eggnog, extract and spices. Pour into prepared pie crust and cover with foil. Bake for 25 minutes, then remove the foil and continue baking for 50-60 minutes or until toothpick inserted in the center comes out clean. Cool completely and refrigerate any leftovers.

Note: Serving size: 1 slice Calories: 300 Fat:13g Carbs: 38g Protein: 5g Nutritional value will change if using sugar substitute.

FLUFFY GELATIN

1 box sugar-free gelatin any flavor free
8 T. frozen whipped topping fat

Make jello according to directions on box. Put in refrigerator to set. Once set, divide gelatin into four 1/2 cup servings. Vigorously mix 2 T. of whipped topping with each 1/2 cup serving.

Note: Calories: 30 Fat: 0 grams Protein: 1 gram Carbs: 2g

HIGH PROTEIN PUMPKIN PROTEIN PUDDING

muschealth.com

1 pkg (1 oz) Butterscotch gelatin
1/2 tsp. pumpkin pie spice
Sugar free instant pudding
1/4 tsp. cinnamon
1 c. skim milk
1/0 tsp. nutmeg
2 scoops protein supplement
1/8 tsp. ginger
1/2 c. canned pumpkin

Measure 1 c. cold skim milk. Add 2 scoops protein to the one cup of cold milk and mix thoroughly by shaking or stirring. Using a fork, blend the dry pudding mix and spices in a bowl. Pour in the protein/milk mixture. Add 1/2 cup canned pumpkin. Stir/beat until thoroughly mixed (a wire whisk or mixer works best). Pour into small container and chill in the fridge. Garnish with a graham cracker and fat free whipped topping.

Note: Calories: 120 Fat: 1g Protein: 9g Carbs: 19g

IMPOSSIBLE COCONUT CUSTARD PIE

Tammy McCoy

1/2 c. Baking mix 1 can (31/2oz) coconut
3/4 c. sugar 1 tsp. vanilla
4 eggs 1 T. butter, softened
2 c. milk

Combine all ingredients and pour into 9 inch buttered pie pan. Bake at 400° degrees for 25-30 minutes until custard sets. Like magic it layers into crust, custard, coconut topping. Cool.

Note: Not a low fat, low sugar food.

LEMON DELIGHT
I stick butter or margarine, melted
8 oz pkg low fat cream cheese, softened
I c. flour
I c. sugar or Splenda®
I I/2 c. pecan, chopped (optional - will be solid food if used)
2 boxes Lemon instant pudding, regular size (made to directions and refrigerated)
I 16oz container frozen whipped topping
Making 4 layers in a 9 x 13 glass dish1st layer - butter, flour and 3/4 cup pecans mixed together and pressed into the bottom of glass dish. Bake at 350 degrees for 10 - 15 min until light brown. Cool completely. 2nd layer - cream cheese, sugar and I cup Cool Whip. Blend until creamy and spread over 1st layer. 3rd layer - Lemon pudding (made to box directions) spread evenly over 2nd layer. 4th layer - extra Cool Whip spread evenly over 3rd layer and topped with remaining pecans. Cover and refrigerate for several hours before serving.
Note: If you omit the pecans, this can be used as a mushy stage treat.

PEANUT BUTTER SUNDAE TOPPING
I/2 c. chunky peanut butter (may use creamy)
I/4 c. water
I/3 c. maple-flavored pancake syrup
In a 1-quart bowl, stir peanut butter and syrup until combined. Gradually stir in water until smooth. Serve over ice cream.

PUMPKIN RICOTTA MOUSSE
muschealth.com
I c. part skim ricotta cheese
2 T. Splenda® (granulated)
I c. pumpkin purée
I/2 tsp. pumpkin pie spice
2 T. sugar-free vanilla instant
I ⅓ c. thawed sugar-free
pudding mix whipped topping
Combine ricotta and pumpkin and blend in a food processor or blender until smooth. Add pudding mix, Splenda®, pumpkin pie spice, and ⅓ cup cool-whip and blend until smooth. Remove from food processor, pour into a bowl, and fold in I cup of cool-whip. Portion out 1/2 cup portions and refrigerate until ready to serve!
Note: 8 (1/2 cup) portions Calories: 50 Fat: 2g Protein: 4g Carbs: 6g

Solid Phase

BLACK BEAN BROWNIES

1 (15.5 oz) can black beans, rinsed and drained
1/2 c. white sugar or substitute with granulated Splenda
3 eggs
1 tsp. instant coffee (optional)
3 T. vegetable oil
1/2 c. milk chocolate chips
1/4 c. cocoa powder (optional)
1 tsp. vanilla extract
Preheat oven to 350 degrees F. Lightly grease an 8x8 square baking
dish. Combine the black beans, eggs, oil, cocoa powder, vanilla extract,
sugar or granulated Splenda®, and instant coffee in a blender; blend
until smooth; pour the mixture into the prepared baking dish. Sprinkle
the chocolate chips over the top of the mixture. Bake in the preheated
oven until the top is dry and the edges start to pull away from the
sides of the pan, about 30 minutes.
Note: 1 brownie ($\frac{1}{16}$th of recipe) Total calories: 126 kcal Total fat:
5g Carbs: 17g Dietary fiber: 3g Sugars: 9g Protein: 4g

BUTTERFINGER® DESSERT

1 prepared angel food cake
4 (2 1/8oz) size Butterfinger®
1 (1oz) pkg fat-free sugar-free candy bars
vanilla pudding mix
1 1/2 c. skim milk
2 (8oz) containers fat-free Cool Whip®
Spray a 9 x 13" pan with cooking spray. Tear angel food cake into bite
size pieces. Prepare pudding with 1-1/2 cups of skim milk and mix with
2 containers of Cool Whip Free. Crush candy bars. Layer 1/2 cake, 1/2
of pudding mixture and 1/2 of crushed Butterfingers. Repeat layer.
Note: Calories: 185; Fat: 3.1g; Carbs: 36.2g; Protein: 4.2g

CARLA'S NO BAKE FREEZER COOKIES
Carla Harrison
1 1/3 jar simply Jiff
3 lrg shredded wheat biscuits
4 oz. sugar free chocolate chips
10 T. old fashioned oats
5 scoops Syntrax® Nectar
5 T. flax meal
Chocolate Truffle
12 oz cream cheese, softened
10 T. chopped walnuts
3 pkts Truvia®
Set aside 2 scoops of protein powder. Combine all remaining ingredients in a large bowl, mix well. Shape into balls or cookies. Dredge in reserved protein powder. Place in freezer for 1 hour. Store in freezer. Makes 43 pieces.

CARLA'S SUGAR FREE COOL WHIP COOKIES
Carla Harrison
1 box sugar free cake mix 1 egg
1 (8 oz) sugar free whipped topping
Mix ingredients. Drop spoonfuls into Truvia® or Splenda® to coat. Bake at 350 for 12 minutes, cool before removing.

DOUBLE LAYER PUMPKIN DESSERT

Bryn Hamilton

2 - 8oz pkgs cream cheese
2 eggs
1/2 c. Splenda®
2/3c. canned pumpkin
1/2 tsp vanilla
1 tsp pumpkin pie spice

Preheat oven to 325 degrees F (165 degrees C). Spray 8 ramekins with Pam or baking spray. In a large bowl, combine cream cheese, Splenda and vanilla. Beat until smooth. Blend in eggs one at a time. Remove 1 cup of batter and spread equally into bottom of 8 ramekins; set aside. Add pumpkin, cinnamon, cloves and nutmeg to the remaining batter and stir gently until well blended. Carefully spread over the batter in the ramekins. Put ramekins in a shallow pan filled partially with water (water bath). Bake in preheated oven for 20-30 minutes, or until center is almost set. Allow to cool, then refrigerate for 3 hours or overnight.

Optional: Top with Land O'Lakes Whipped Cream with Splenda.

Note: Each serving contains 3 carbohydrates

HIGH PROTEIN SINGLE SERVE BROWNIE

1 scoop protein powder (chocolate 32g)
1 lrg egg
nonfat cooking spray
1/3c. frozen whipped topping, thawed

Spray a mug with cooking spray. Crack egg into mug. Add whipped topping, mix until smooth. Add protein powder, mix until smooth (add water if needed). Microwave on high for 2 minutes (more if needed). Turn mug upside down to drop brownie onto a plate (cut to see if fully cooked). Let cool and enjoy.

Note: Total Fat 18g Total Carbohydrate 23g Dietary Fiber 6g Sugars 11g Protein 41g

HOMEMADE APPLE PIE

Dianna Gill
6-8 green granny smith apples (peeled, cored and sliced)
2 T. all purpose flour
1/2 tsp. ground nutmeg
1 c. Splenda®
2 unbaked pie shells
1/2 c. brown sugar
1/2 stick of butter or margarine
2 tsp. ground cinnamon
Preheat oven to 400°. Cut peeled apples into 1/4 inch slices. In a mixing bowl, combine sugars, cinnamon, flour, nutmeg and a dash of salt. Unroll 1 crust & line into a 9" deep pie pan. Place apples in the crust. Sprinkle the apples with sugar mixture until well coated. Place small slices of butter on top of the apple filling. Fit top crust over the apples. Wet clean hands & dampen the top of pie crust. Press crust down gently & cut 3-4 slits in the top to allow steam to escape pie while cooking. Sprinkle top with additional sugars. Bake pie in preheated oven for 15-20 minutes @ 400 degrees, then reduce heat to 350° & bake for an additional 30 or until crust is lightly golden brown.
Note: Not a low fat food.

OATMEAL & BANANA BREAKFAST COOKIES

2 c. oatmeal (old fashioned or quick is fine)
1/3 c. grapeseed or olive oil
1 tsp. vanilla
3 overripe bananas, mashed
1 c. dried fruit, chopped if necessary
Mix all ingredients in a large bowl. Drop by tablespoonfuls onto greased cookie sheet. Bake at 350° for 20 minutes or until lightly browned on top. Store in airtight container.
Note: High in fiber and only has natural sugars.

PEACH PIE

I c. sugar or Splenda®
4 T. apricot gelatin
I c. water
4-6 lrg peaches, sliced thin
3 T. cornstarch

Mix the sugar, water and cornstarch on stove until clear. Add gelatin and mix until dissolved. Cook until it starts to congeal. Add peaches. Pour into a baked pie shell. Keep refrigerated.

PEANUT BUTTER PIE

I (9 inch) unbaked pie crust (or use graham cracker crust)
I sm. box instant vanilla pudding
I/2 c. peanut butter
I I/2c. milk
3/4 c. powdered sugar (or sugar substitute)
Frozen whipped topping, thawed

Mix peanut butter and powdered sugar until crumbly. Cover bottom of crust with half of the peanut butter crumbs. Make pudding with I1/2 cups milk; pour into crust. Cover pudding with whipped topping and sprinkle remaining crumbs on top of whipped topping. Put in refrigerator to set.

PECAN PIE BITES

Jennifer and Sue at 7 Bites
1 c. honey
2 tsp vanilla
1 c. agave nectar
6 whole eggs
1 c. sugar substitute of choice
2 c. chopped pecans
For Crust:
1 stick butter
2 1/4 c. almond meal (almond flour)

For the crust: Cut the butter into smaller pieces. Put it and the almond meal into the food processor and pulse until mixture resembles sand. Press into a 9 x 13 glass baking dish.For the filling:In a large bowl, combine eggs, honey, agave nectar, vanilla, and sugar substitute with whisk until well combined. Pour into crust and sprinkle pecans over the top. Bake at 325° for 40-45 minutes. Check by shaking the dish. If it doesn't jiggle, it's ready. If it still wiggles, leave in for 5 minutes at a time until done. Once done, allow to cool for 15-20 minutes to finish setting, then cut into 1 x 1 in pieces. You can wrap and freeze them in individual servings - just take them out about 30 minutes before you're going to indulge!

8 THIS AND THAT

CRISPY SHRIMP BURGERS

slenderkitchen.com
1 lb. shrimp, peeled and deveined
1 tsp. onion powder
pinch cayenne pepper
2 garlic cloves
1/2 c. Panko breadcrumbs
1/8 c. cilantro or parsley
1 egg, lightly beaten
1 tsp. salt
1 T. vegetable oil
1 tsp. paprika
Take half the shrimp and coarsely chop it. Add it to a bowl. Take the
other half and add it to a food processor with the garlic and cilantro.
Pulse to create a chunky paste. Mix in with the chopped shrimp. Add
the salt, paprika, onion powder, cayenne pepper, Panko breadcrumbs,
and egg. Mix until just combine. Divide into four patties. Heat a skillet
over medium high heat with the vegetable oil. Add the burgers and
cook for 3-4 minutes on each side. Serve on a roll as a burger,
wrapped in lettuce, or as a burger bowl.
Note: 194.7 calories, 6.7g of fat, 6.9g of carbs,.7g of fiber, 25.3g of
protein

HOMEMADE RANCH SEASONING MIX
1/2 c. dry buttermilk
2 tsp. dried chives
1 T. dried parsley, crushed
1/2 - 1 tsp. salt
2 tsp. dried dill weed
1/2 tsp. garlic powder
2 tsp. onion powder
1/4 tsp. ground pepper
1 tsp. dried onion flakes

Mix all of the spices together and store in an airtight container. To make a quick and easy ranch dressing, mix 3/4 cup non fat Greek yogurt or sour cream and 1 tbsp of homemade ranch seasoning. If you want a thinner dressing, mix in 1/3 to 1/4 cup skim milk.
Note: calories: under 20.

HOMEMADE TACO SEASONING
1 part chili powder
1 part onion powder
1 part ground cumin
1/4 - 1/2 part crushed red pepper
1 part garlic powder

Mix all the spices together and store in an airtight container.

SUGAR FREE BBQ SAUCE
Denise at muschealth.com
1 small onion, minced
3 T. Worcestershire sauce
1 clove garlic, minced
1/2 tsp. ground cloves
1 (6 oz) can tomato paste
1 tsp. hot sauce
1 (12 oz) can diet soda
1/2 c. water
1/4 c. low-carb ketchup
1 tsp. Liquid Smoke®

Spray some cooking spray in a 2 quart pan. Add minced onion and cook over medium heat until soft (3-5 min). Add minced garlic and stir for 1 minute. Add the tomato paste, diet soda, ketchup, mustard, Worcestershire, ground cloves, Tabasco/hot sauce, and 1/2 c. water; Stir well. Simmer for 20-30 minutes. Add 1 tsp. Liquid Smoke before serving. Store in a glass bottle for serving.
Note: 10 (1/4 c. servings) Cals: 20 Fat: 0g Protein: 1g Carb:5g

SUGAR FREE PUMPKIN APPLE BUTTER

1 (15oz) can Libby's® 100% Pure Pumpkin Purée
1 T. molasses
1 1/2 tsp. pumpkin pie spice (or 1 tsp. cinnamon, 1/2 tsp.
ginger, pinch ground clove)
1 apple, peeled and grated
1/2 c. Truvia® Baking Blend
1/2 tsp. vanilla
1/8 tsp. salt

Blend together the pumpkin, apple, Truvia, molasses, vanilla, pumpkin pie spice and salt in a medium saucepan. Bring to a boil over medium high heat. Reduce heat and simmer for 60 minutes, stirring occasionally, until thick and velvety. Store in covered container in the refrigerator.

WHIPPED CREAM FROSTING (SUGAR FREE)

Carla Harrison
1 (8 oz) pkg reduced-fat cream cheese, softened
1 tsp vanilla extract
1/2 tsp almond extract
1/2 c. Splenda®
2 c. of heavy cream

Combine the cream cheese, sugar, vanilla extract and almond extract in a large mixing bowl or the bowl of your mixer. Once all in the bowl, mix on medium speed until smooth. While the mixture is still whipping, slowly pour in the heavy cream. Stop and scrape the bottom of the bowl a few times while you continue whipping until the cream can hold a stiff peak.

Note: This recipe makes 5 cups

Liquid Phase

LOW CARB BBQ SAUCE
Carla Harrison
12 oz tomato paste
1/4 c. Brown Sugar Twin
3 T. Worcestershire sauce
1 T. garlic powder
1 T. lemon juice
1 tsp. onion powder
2 T. vinegar
1/2 c. water
4 pkts Splenda®
In a medium saucepan, combine all ingredients. Bring to a boil. Reduce heat to medium-low and simmer, covered, for 30- 45 minutes, uncover &
reduce to consistency you like.
Note: Makes just under 3 cups.

Mushy Phase

JULIE'S TUNA AND WHITE BEAN SPREAD
Julie at muschealth.com
5 oz tuna canned in water, drained
1 T. olive oil
1 T. lemon juice
16 oz. canned white beans or cannellini beans, drained and rinsed
1/4 c. flat leaf parsley, chopped
Garlic and salt to taste
In a blender or food processor with the knife blade attached, whirl the tuna, beans, olive oil, lemon juice and parsley until smooth. Add garlic and salt to taste. Serve with crudités such as sliced cucumber, bell pepper, carrots, celery and jicama or spread on a low-carb tortilla and roll it up.
Note: Yields: 8, 1/4 cup servings Calories: 90 Fat: 2.5 g (0 g saturated) Protein: 8 g Carb: 9 g (3 g fiber)

PHILADELPHIA HOLLANDAISE

1 (8oz) pkg. cream cheese, cubed
2 egg yolks
2 T. lemon juice
1/2 c. milk dash of salt

Heat cream cheese and milk over low heat; stir until smooth. Blend in egg yolks, lemon juice and salt. Serve over hot cooked vegetables.
Note: Yield: 1 3/4 cups

PIZZA SAUCE

1 (48 oz) can tomato juice
1 T. garlic powder
1 (12 oz) can tomato paste
1 T. onion flakes
3 T. Parmesan cheese, grated
1 T. pepper
2 bay leaves
1 T. oregano
1 T. sweet basil

Put all the ingredients in a saucepan and cook until thick. Remove bay leaves. Pour into an 8-inch jar and cover tightly with lid. Put jars into the freezer. When you are ready to make the pizza, thaw the sauce.

SUGAR-FREE STRAWBERRY JAM

3/4 c. diet lemon-lime soda
1 1/2 tsp. lemon juice
1 (3 oz) pkg. sugar-free strawberry flavored gelatin
1 c. mashed, fresh or unsweetened frozen strawberries

In a saucepan, bring soda to a boil. Remove from the heat; stir in gelatin until dissolved. Stir in strawberries and lemon juice. Pour into jars or plastic containers; cover and refrigerate up to 3 weeks. Do not freeze.

SUSAN'S LITE GODDESS DRESSING
Susan at muschealth.com
6 oz. lite firm silken tofu (1/2 pkg of Mori-Nu®)
1/4 tsp. sesame oil
1 T. tahini
1/4 c. water
2 green onions, white parts
1 1/2 T. cider vinegar removed, chopped
2 T. lemon juice
1 T. chopped fresh parsley, packed
2 tsp. low-sodium soy sauce
1/2 tsp. salt
1 lrg clove garlic
Place all ingredients in blender and process until smooth.
Note: Yields: 10 servings, 2 Tbsp each Calories: 20 Fat: 1g Protein: 1g Carb: 1g

Solid Phase

CAJUN SPICED NUTS
Jennifer and Sue at 7 Bites
4 c. mixed nuts
1/4 tsp. black pepper
1 egg white
1/4 tsp. garlic powder
1 T. water
1/4 tsp. cumin
2 tsp. cajun seasoning or 1/4 tsp. sea salt
1/4 tsp. chili powder
1/4 tsp cayenne pepper
In a bowl, combine egg white, water and seasoning until well combined. Put nuts and seasoning mix into a large (1 gallon) sized plastic storage bag and massage until well coated. Pour onto a parchment-lined baking sheet and flatten into a single layer. Bake at 325° for 30-40 minutes.

CARLA'S POWER BALLS

Carla Harrison
1 Jar peanut butter (no sugar added)
1 c. chopped nuts (walnuts or pecans)
5 scoops chocolate protein powder (or vanilla)
6 pkts. Truvia® or other sweetener
6 T. sugar free maple syrup
1 c. flax meal
Fold all ingredients, except flax meal, into a bowl with a pastry blender; blend until mixed well. Roll into walnut sized balls, then roll in flax meal. Makes approximately 70 power balls.

CINNAMON SPICED NUTS

Jennifer and Sue at 7 Bites
2 c. mixed nuts
1 T. water
1 T. honey
1/4 tsp cinnamon
1 T. vegetable oil
2 T. sugar substitute
Combine honey, oil, water, cinnamon and sugar substitute in a large (1 gallon sized) plastic storage bag. Add nuts and massage until well coated. Turn out onto parchment-lined baking sheet and flatten into a single layer. Bake at 325 for 30-40 minutes.

REBECCA'S P-NUT BUTTER CRUNCH

Rebecca at muschealth.com
1 Quaker rice cake, plain
1 T. dry roasted sunflower seeds
1 T. Smucker®'s Natural cream
peanut butter
cinnamon to taste
1 T. Polander® Strawberry All Fruit
Spread peanut butter on top of rice cake, followed by All Fruit and then sprinkle seeds and cinnamon on top. Yum!
Note: Calories: 230 Total Fat: 13g Carbs: 22g Protein: 7g

BONUS RECIPES

DIET V8 SPLASH DRINK
Mary Bayones
6-8 oz diet v8 splash drink
1 scoop unflavored protein powder
Mix until well blended.

LOW CALORIE MANDARIN ORANGE SALAD
Mary Bayones
1 box sugar free orange jello
8 oz low fat cottage cheese
1 container lite cool whip
1 sm can mandarin oranges drained
Prepare Jello by following directions on box. (by boiling one cup water and dissolving jello and add one cup cold water) do not refrigerate yet. Combine jello mix, cottage cheese, cool whip and oranges until well blended. Refrigerate until dish is set or at least 6 hours.

CRAB DIP
8 oz light cream cheese softened
1/3 cup light mayo
1/2 tsp seasoned salt
1 1/2 T. dried minced onion
1 tsp prepared mustard or horseradish
1 T. chopped parsley (dried)
dash garlic powder
1 6 oz can crab meat
Fresh raw veggies for dipping
Blend together cream cheese, mayo, mustard, onion, and seasoned salt. Fold in parsley, garlic powder and crab meat.

CHICKEN AND SWEET ONION CASSEROLE

3-4 boneless skinless chicken breast halves
3-4 large red skinned or Yukon gold potatoes peeled and sliced 1/4 inch thick
3-4 medium Vidalia sweet onions peeled and sliced ¼ inch thick
1 can low sodium condensed cream of mushroom soup
1/4 c. plain yogurt
1/4 c. chicken broth
8 oz. sliced mushrooms
salt, pepper and paprika

Preheat oven to 350^F . In a bottom of a 2 qt casserole dish, layer the potatoes, mushrooms, onion and chicken. Salt and pepper to taste. In a small bowl combine, the condensed soup, yogurt and broth. Pour over casserole ingredients. Sprinkle with paprika. Cover casserole and bake one hour. Allow to stand at room temp for 5-10 mins then enjoy.

THREE BEAN SALAD

1 can garbanzo beans, drained and rinsed
1 can kidney beans, drained and rinsed
1 can black beans, drained and rinsed
½ small onion, finely chopped
1 lrg tomato, finely chopped
1 c. green olives, thinly sliced
1 c. black olives, thinly sliced
½ bunch fresh dill, finely chopped
3 cloves garlic, minced
½ c. olive oil
4 T. lemon juice
salt and pepper to taste

Place all ingredients in large mixing bowl and blend well. Marinate overnight. Serve chilled.

BARSZCZ (POLISH BEET SOUP)

Agatha Wolkowicz

6 beets
1 carrot
1 small onion
2 potatoes
1 garlic clove
1 Bouilon cube
1 lemon
fresh dill
Flour
Sour cream

Prep:
Use gloves, beets stain.
Chop garlic and onion
Wash beets and green stem
Chop stem and leaves
Peel beets and then dice (or shred) into small cubes
Peel and chop potato into small cubes
Peel and dice carrot
Mix 2 tablespoons of sour cream with 1 tablespoon of flour into separate cup

Steps
Add garlic and onion into soup pot, sauté over olive oil on low heat
Add beets with stem and leaves to pot Add carrots and potatoes
Fill pot with water. Let boil. Add 1 Bullion cube. Squeeze of lemon (2 tablespoons). 2 tablespoons of wine vinegar. Pinch of salt. Pinch of pepper. Add sour cream and flour mixture to soup. Now let boil for 10 minutes. Add ¼ tablespoon dill. Serve over hard boiled egg (sliced into quarters).

DILL PICKLE SOUP

Agatha Wolkowicz

3/4 large white onion
I carrot
2 garlic cloves
2 large potatoes
2 liters of vegetable or chicken broth
4-5 Polish pickles
Half cup of pickle juice (from pickle container)
Fresh dill
Parsley
Salt & Pepper
Pouring cream
Sour cream
Stick of butter

Olive oil

Prep:
Chop up potatoes, onion, and carrots into small pieces
Dice garlic
Grate pickles

Steps:
Add half stick of butter into saucepan with tablespoon olive oil
Sauté onions and carrots (3-5 minutes). Add garlic and potatoes (stir
for 3-5 minutes). Add vegetable or chicken broth (stir well, cover, and
let sit for 10 minutes) When boiling, add grated pickles, pickle juice.
Then add I teaspoon dill, ¼ teaspoon parsley, ¼ teaspoon salt, pinch
of pepper. Mix in well. When potatoes soft, add 4 tablespoons of
pouring cream. Stir well. Add large spoonful of sour cream. Stir well.

MINESTRONE SOUP
Kathy White
4 oz smoked ham, diced
2 carrots, peeled and diced
I onion, diced
2 potatoes, peeled and diced
I celery stalk, diced
I leek, sliced, white part only
2 T. olive oil
I qt. water
2 beef bouillon cubes
2 T. tomato paste
I clove garlic, minced
I cup orzo pasta
1/3 c. long grain white rice
I tsp dried basil
I tsp dried thyme
I (14.5 oz) can diced tomatoes
10 oz frozen peas, thawed
salt and pepper to taste

In a large skillet, sauté ham and vegetables in oil for several minutes. Transfer into a large stock pot. Add water, bouillon cubes, tomato paste, garlic, orzo, rice, basil and thyme. Cook, covered, on medium heat for 20 minutes. Add tomatoes and peas to soup. Simmer on low heat for 10 minutes. Add salt and pepper to taste. Puree for mushy phase, strain for liquid phase.

ITALIAN STYLE SQUASH
Kathy White
2 medium zucchini squash, cut lengthwise in half then crosswise into 1/2 inch pieces
I large onion, sliced and separated into rings
2 T. firm margarine or butter, cut into small pieces
I tsp salt
1/2 tsp Italian seasoning
1/8 tsp pepper
2 cloves garlic, finely chopped

Mix all ingredients in 2 quart casserole dish. Cover and microwave on high 3 minutes; stir. Cover and microwave until vegetables are crisp – tender, 4-5 minutes.

SPICY ASIAN COCKTAIL SHRIMP
Kathy White
1-1/2 lbs raw medium shrimp, peeled
3 green onions, chopped
1/4 c. lime juice
1 T reduced sodium soy sauce
2 T rice vinegar
1/4 tsp black pepper
1/8 tsp ground red pepper
2 garlic cloves, finely chopped
1 T. fresh ginger, minced
1 T. sesame seeds
2 T. sesame oil

Mix all ingredients except oil in large glass or plastic bowl. Cover and refrigerate for 4 hours. Heat oven to 400 degrees. Spray 13x9 pan with nonstick cooking spray. Arrange shrimp in single layer. Bake 10 to 12 minutes or until shrimp is pink. Drizzle with oil. Serve hot with toothpicks. Makes 12 servings.

CHICKEN SPRING ROLLS
Kathy White
2 c. pre-shredded coleslaw mix
1 c. cooked chicken, finely chopped
1 c. water chestnuts, finely chopped
8 green onions, thinly sliced
6 T. plum sauce, divided
2 tsp sesame oil
1 pkg egg roll wrappers

Combine coleslaw, chicken, water chestnuts, onions, 4 tablespoons of plum sauce and sesame oil in medium bowl; mix well. Spread the remaining 2 tablespoons of plum sauce evenly over wrappers. Spread about 1/2 cup coleslaw mixture on each wrapper to within 1/4 inch of edge; fold up according to package instructions. Wrap tightly in plastic wrap. Refrigerate at least 1 hour or up to 24 hours before serving. Bake on ungreased cookie sheet for 10-12 minutes at 350 degrees or until golden brown. Makes 12 appetizers.

CRANBERRY MEATBALLS

Kathy White
2 lbs ground beef
1 tsp salt
1 tsp pepper
1/2 tsp dried oregano
1 tsp dried onion flakes
1 tsp Parmesan cheese
1/2 c. dried bread crumbs
Sauce:
1-1/2 c. chili sauce
12 oz jellied cranberry sauce
2 tsp lemon juice
2 T. brown sugar

To prepare meatballs, combine ground beef, salt, pepper, oregano, onion flakes, Parmesan cheese and bread crumbs in a large mixing bowl. Form into 1 inch balls. Either bake in oven at 375 degrees for 20 minutes or fry until cooked through. Set aside. To prepare the sauce, combine chili sauce, cranberry sauce, lemon juice and brown sugar in a sauce pan. Cook over medium heat until jelly is melted. Place meatballs in sauce, cover pan and allow to simmer on low for 30 minutes.

RICOTTA CROSTINI

Kathy White
1 c. Italian seasoned bread crumbs
1 c. nonfat ricotta cheese
2 egg whites
1 T. dried basil
1/2 tsp salt
1/4 tsp pepper
1 clove garlic, finely chopped
24 slices day-old French bread, 1/4 inch thick
2 tomatoes, seeded and diced
1/4 c. Parmesan cheese, grated

Mix bread crumbs, ricotta cheese, egg whites, basil, salt, pepper, and garlic. Preheat oven to broil. Spread about 1 tablespoon ricotta mixture on each bread slice. Sprinkle with 2 tsps of tomatoes and 1/2 tsp parmesan cheese. Broil with tops about 6 inches away from heat for three minutes or until bubbly. Serve Hot.

RED, WHITE AND GREEN BEANS
Kathy White
1 lb green beans, cut into 1-inch pieces
1/4 c. red bell peppers, roasted and chopped
2 T. butter or margarine, melted
1 T. lemon juice
2 tsp Dijon mustard
2 tsp honey
1/2 tsp pepper
1 tsp soy sauce
1 16 oz can great northern or navy beans, rinsed and drained

Boil green beans in medium saucepan for 5 minutes. Drain water. Stir in remaining ingredients. Cook over medium heat for about 5 minutes, stirring occasionally, until hot. Makes 4 servings.

CREAMY DILLED CARROTS AND ONIONS
Kathy White
1 c. pearl onions
3 c. carrots
3/4 c. water
1 T. butter or margarine
1/2 tsp salt
1/4 tsp sugar or sugar substitute
pinch of white pepper
1 T. all purpose flour
1/2 c. light cream
2 tsp dill weed, dried

In a small saucepan, boil onions for 3 minutes. Drain and set aside until onions are cool enough to handle. Peel onions. In a large saucepan, combine carrots, onions, water, butter, salt, sugar and pepper. Cover and simmer until carrots are crisp-tender, about 10 minutes. Drain liquid into a small saucepan; set the carrots and onions aside and keep warm. Bring liquid to a boil. In a small bowl, combine flour and cream until smooth; slowly add to liquid, stirring constantly. Simmer for 10 minutes, stirring occasionally. Pour over the onions and carrots; stir in dill weed. Cover and let stand for 15 minutes before serving.

TWICE-BAKED NEW POTATOES
Kathy White
1-1/2 lbs red potatoes
2 T. vegetable oil
1 c. shredded cheddar cheese
1/2 c. sour cream
3 oz cream cheese, softened
1/3 c. green onions, minced
1 garlic clove, minced
1/2 tsp basil, dried
1/2 tsp salt and pepper
1/2 lb sliced bacon, cooked and crumbled

Pierce potatoes; rub skins with oil. Place in baking pan. Bake uncovered at 400 degrees for 50 minutes or until tender. Allow to cool to the touch. In a mixing bowl, combine cheddar cheese, sour cream, cream cheese, onions, basil, garlic, salt and pepper. Cut potatoes in half; carefully scoop out pulp, leaving a thin shell. Add pulp to the cheese mixture and mash; stir in bacon. Stuff potato shells. Broil for 7-8 minutes or until heated through.

HOT PINEAPPLE CASSEROLE
Kathy White
2 large cans pineapple chunks, drained
6 T. flour
1 c. sugar or granulated sugar substitute
2 c. shredded cheddar cheese
1 c. crumbled butter flavored crackers
1 stick margarine, melted

Mix pineapple chunks, flour and sugar; stir in cheese and pour into buttered casserole dish. Cover with crumbs, then pour melted margarine over casserole. Bake 20-25 minutes at 325 degrees.

ROASTED WINTER VEGETABLES

Kathy White
1/2 c. butter or margarine
2 T. fresh sage leaves, chopped or 2 tsp. dried sage leaves
2 cloves garlic, finely chopped
1/2 lb brussel sprouts, halved
1/2 lb parsnips, peeled and cut into 2-inch pieces
1/4 lb carrots, cut into ½-inch rounds
1 small butternut squash, peeled, seeded and cut into 1-inch pieces
1/2 lb turnips, peeled and cut into 8 wedges

Heat oven to 375 degrees. Melt butter in 1 quart saucepan over medium heat; stir in sage and garlic. Place remaining ingredients in 13x9 pan. Pour butter mixture over vegetables; stir to coat. Season with salt and pepper. Cover and bake 25 to 30 minutes, stirring occasionally, until vegetables are crisp-tender. Makes 4 servings.

CRANBERRY SALAD

Kathy White
2 c. fresh cranberries
1 orange, peeled and diced
1 c. sugar
1 pkg orange gelatin
1/2 c. celery, chopped
1/2 c. nuts, chopped
1/2 c. apples, chopped

Puree cranberries and orange in a food processor. Stir in one cup of sugar and let stand 2 or 3 hours. Prepare one package of orange gelatin with one cup boiling water and cool. When gelatin begins to set, combine all ingredients and pour into mold.

SWEET POTATO PUDDING
Kathy White
2 eggs, beaten
3/4 c. sugar or sugar substitute
2 cups grated raw sweet potatoes
1 (13 oz) can evaporated milk
1/2 c. milk
1/2 tsp cinnamon
1/2 tsp salt
1/2 c. margarine, melted
1 c. flaked coconut

Combine eggs and sugar in large mixing bowl, beat well; stir in remaining ingredients. Pour into a greased 1-1/2 quart casserole dish. Bake at 350 degrees for 1 hour. Makes 6-8 servings.

CEASAR GREEN BEANS
Kathy White
1 (20 oz) pkg frozen cut green beans
2 T. salad oil
1 T. vinegar
1 T. minced onion
1 clove garlic, crushed
2 T. bread crumbs
2 T. Parmesan cheese
1 T. butter, melted

Cook beans as directed, drain. Toss with salad oil, vinegar, onion, and garlic. Pour into ungreased casserole dish. Stir together bread crumbs, cheese and melted butter. Sprinkle over beans. Bake at 350 degrees for 15-20 minutes.

ORANGE STUFFED YAMS

Kathy White
6 medium yams
3 T. butter or margarine
1/4 tsp. salt
2 T. brown sugar (or brown sugar substitute)
1/2 tsp. cinnamon
1/2 c. orange sections, diced
1/4 c. flaked coconut
1/2 tsp lemon rind, grated

Bake yams at 400 degrees for 35-40 minutes or until soft. Cut slice from top of each yam and scoop out insides keeping shell intact. Mash yams with butter. Add salt, brown sugar, cinnamon, orange sections, coconut and lemon rind. Mix well. Spoon into shells and bake at 400 degrees for 15 minutes or until lightly browned.

CREAMY COTTAGE CHEESE CASSEROLE

Kathy White
1 (16 oz) pkg wide egg noodles
2 c. cottage cheese
1/4 c. sour cream
1/4 c. onions
2 T. green pepper
2 T. flour
1 can of spam
3/4 tsp salt, omit if you want
1/2 tsp sugar
1/8 tsp pepper
2 c. tomato sauce

Prepare noodles according to package instructions and set aside. Mix together cottage cheese, sour cream, onions, green peppers and flour. Spread half of the noodles in a 11x7 baking dish. Spread the cheese mixture over the noodles. Cover with remaining noodles, combine remaining ingredients and pour over noodles. Bake in moderate oven at 350 degrees, until heated through, about 30 minutes.

PUMPKIN TORTE

Kathy White

3 c. graham cracker crumbs
1/2 c. butter, softened
1-3/4 c. sugar, divided
1 (8 oz) pkg cream cheese, softened
2 eggs
2 c. canned pumpkin
3 eggs, separated
1/2 c. milk
1 tsp cinnamon
1/2 tsp salt
1 envelope gelatin
1/4 c. water
whipped topping, optional

Combine graham cracker, butter and 1/4 cup sugar and press into 13x9 pan. Mix cream cheese, 3/4 cup sugar and 2 beaten eggs until creamy. Spoon over crust and bake at 350 degrees for 20 minutes. In saucepan, combine canned pumpkin, 3 egg yolks, milk, 1/2 cup sugar, cinnamon and salt. Cook over medium heat until thick. Add gelatin and water to cooked pumpkin mixture and let cool completely. Beat 3 egg whites with 1/4 cup sugar. Fold into cooled pumpkin mixture and pour over baked crust. Top with whipped topping.

CHERRY COBBLER

Kathy White

1-1/2 c flour
1-1/2 c sugar or granulated sugar substitute such as Splenda®
3/4 c. milk
3 tsp baking powder
3 T. shortening
2 cans cherry pie filling

Mix first fix ingredients well to form crust. Place 2 cans cherry pie filling in pie pan and spread crust on top. Bake at 350 degrees for 45 minutes or until golden brown.

BROCCOLI SALAD

Kathy White
Salad:
1 head broccoli, chopped
8 oz. sharp cheddar cheese, shredded
8 oz. bacon, cooked and crumbled
1 medium purple onion, sliced thin
1 c. raisins
1 c. pecans, chopped
1 c. pineapple, drained and crushed
Dressing:
1/2 c. mayonnaise
1 T. red wine vinegar
1/4 c. sugar substitute

Combine salad ingredients in a large bowl. Whisk together dressing ingredients. Pour dressing over salad and refrigerate overnight.

EGGPLANT PARMEGIANA

Kathy White
2 medium eggplants
salt to taste
1 jar Ragu Italian sauce
6 oz shredded mozzarella cheese
1/4 c. grated Parmesan cheese
1 c. cooking oil

Soak sliced eggplant in salty water for 30 minutes. Drain dry on paper towel. Brush each slice with cooking oil. Flour. Cook until lightly browned. Drain on paper towel. Spread 1/2 cup Ragu over bottom of a 2 quart casserole dish. Arrange a layer of eggplant. Sprinkle with Mozzarella and Parmesan cheese. Combine all ingredients. Pour into a 2 quart casserole dish. Bake in a 350 degree oven, covered for 20 minutes. Uncover for 20 minutes longer.

CHICKEN TETRAZZINI
Kathy White
I lb spaghetti
Chicken broth
1/2 c. chopped celery
3 T. butter
I can sliced mushrooms
I can mushroom soup
I 1/2 tsp Greek seasoning
I 1/2 lb Velveeta cheese, cubed
salt and pepper to taste
I soup can milk
I large chicken, cooked and chopped
Parmesan cheese

Cook spaghetti in broth until tender and drain. Sauté celery in butter. Mix or add all ingredients except Parmesan cheese. Pour into a 13x9 casserole dish. Sprinkle Parmesan cheese on top. Bake at 350 degrees for 45 minutes.

BROCCOLI AND CHEESE SOUP
Kathy White
I head fresh broccoli, washed
1/3 c butter
I small onion, chopped
2 cloves garlic, minced
1/3 c flour
2 c. half and half or light cream
2 c. chicken broth
I tsp. Worcestershire sauce
salt and pepper to taste
2 c. sharp cheddar cheese, grated
1/4 c. green onions, chopped

Cut the florets off the stalk and into bite-sized pieces. Melt butter in a saucepan and sauté broccoli, onion and garlic until tender. Combine flour and half and half or cream; stir until smooth. Gradually add to broccoli. Add chicken broth, Worcestershire sauce, salt and pepper; stir until thickened. Add cheese and stir over low heat until cheese is melted. Serve warm with chopped green onions for garnish, if desired.

ENGLISH PEA SALAD

Kathy White
4 slices bacon
1 (10 oz) pkg frozen peas, thawed and drained
1 c. shredded cheddar
2 hard-cooked eggs, peeled and chopped
3 T. mayonnaise
2 tsp freshly squeezed lemon juice
salt and pepper to taste

In a large skillet, cook the bacon over medium heat until crisp. Transfer to a paper towel-lined plate to drain. Let cool. In a medium serving bowl, combine the bacon, peas, cheese, and eggs. Stir in the mayonnaise, lemon juice and salt immediately or refrigerate until ready to serve.

TACO SOUP

Kathy White
Chopped green onions
Grated cheese
Sour cream
Corn chips
1 (1 oz) pkg ranch salad dressing mix
1 (1.25 oz) pkg taco seasoning mix
1/2 c. green olives, sliced (optional)
1 small can black olives, drained and sliced (optional)
2 (4.5 oz) cans diced green chilies
1 (14.5 oz) can tomatoes with chilies
1 (14.5 oz) can Mexican tomatoes
1 (15.25 oz) can whole kernel corn, drained
1 (15.5 oz) can pink kidney beans
2 (15.5 oz) cans pinto beans
2 c. diced onions
2 lbs ground beef, browned

Place browned ground beef and onions in skillet and warm. When warm, transfer to stockpot or crockpot. Add the beans, corn, green onions, tomatoes, chilies, olives, and seasonings, and cook on low setting all day (6-8 hours) if using a crockpot, or simmer over low heat for about 1 hour in a stock pot on the stove. To serve, place a few corn chips in each bowl and ladle soup over them. Top with sour cream, cheese and jalapenos.

SPINACH AND STRAWBERRY SALAD
Kathy White
1 (10 – 12 oz) pkg baby spinach, washed and dried
1/3 c. sliced almonds, toasted
1 qt strawberries, hulled and quartered
1 whole cucumber, peeled, seeded, and finely diced
Dressing:
Juice of half a lemon
2 T. white wine vinegar
1/3 c. sugar
1 T. vegetable oil
1 tsp. poppy seeds

In a large salad bowl, add the spinach, almonds, strawberries, and cucumber and toss together. For the dressing: In a small glass bowl or jar with a tight fitting lid, combine the lemon juice, vinegar, sugar, oil and poppy seeds. Whisk together in a glass bowl or shake if using a jar. Dress the salad right before serving.

TRUE OLD FASHIONED PEACH COBBLER
Kathy White
Fruit:
2 1/2 c. sliced fresh peaches
2 T. butter
1 c. fruit juice (orange juice works well)
3/4 c. sugar or granulated Splenda®
Heat the above ingredients until warm and sugar is dissolved. You will pour the peach mixture on top of the batter.
Batter:
1/4 c. Butter
1 c. sugar or granulated Splenda®
3/4 c. flour
1 tsp. baking powder
1/2 c. milk
1/2 tsp. salt
Beat together until smooth.
Spoon batter into a greased, deep baking dish. Top with fruit mixture. Batter will rise up through the fruit giving all a delicious flavor. Bake 45-55 min at 400 degrees until golden and bubbly. Serve each serving with a little milk or cream or vanilla ice cream or cool whip on top.

OLD-TIME BEEF STEW
Kathy White
2 lb Stew meat
2 T. vegetable oil
2 c. water
1 tsp. Worcestershire sauce
1 garlic clove, peeled
1 or 2 bay leaves
1 medium onion, sliced
1 tsp. salt
1 tsp. sugar
1/2 tsp. pepper
1/2 tsp. paprika
dash ground allspice or ground cloves
3 large carrots, sliced
4 red potatoes, quartered
3 ribs celery, chopped
2 T. cornstarch

Brown meat in hot oil. Add water, Worcestershire sauce, garlic, bay leaves, onion, salt, sugar, pepper, paprika, and allspice. Cover and simmer 1 1/2 hours. Remove bay leaves and garlic clove. Add carrots, potatoes, and celery. Cover and cook 30 to 40 minutes longer. To thicken gravy, remove 2 cups hot liquid. Using a separate bowl, combine 1/4 cup water and cornstarch until smooth. Mix with hot liquid and return mixture to pot. Stir and cook until bubbly.

STRAWBERRY SALAD
Kathy White
1 lrg pkg strawberry gelatin
1 c. frozen strawberries
1 c. chopped pecans
1/2 pint sour cream

Dissolve gelatin in 1 cup hot water; add 2 cups cold water; add strawberries and pecans and stir. Pour half of gelatin mixture into mold. Place half-filled mold in fridge until congealed. Let remaining mixture thicken in refrigerator but don't let it congeal. Spread sour cream on congealed mixture in mold. Pour remaining thickened gelatin mixture over sour cream and refrigerate until firm.

PULLED CHICKEN SANDWICHES

Kathy White
3 c. thinly sliced onion
1 tsp. canola oil
1 3/4 lb. skinless, boneless chicken breast halves
1 c. ketchup
2 T. cider vinegar
2 T. molasses
1 T. Dijon mustard
1 tsp. onion powder
1 tsp. ground cumin
1/2 tsp. garlic powder
1/2 tsp. hot sauce
8 (1.2 oz) whole-wheat hamburger buns - toasted

Place onion in a 4 quart oval slow cooker. Heat a large nonstick skillet over medium high heat. Add oil to pan; swirl to coat. Add half of chicken and cook 3 to 4 minutes on each side until golden brown. Place chicken in a single layer on top of onion. Repeat procedure with remaining chicken. Combine ketchup and next 7 ingredients (through hot sauce); pour over chicken. Cover and cook on LOW for 4 hours until chicken is tender and sauce is thick. Remove chicken from cooker. Shred chicken with 2 forks and stir into sauce. Spoon 3/4 cup chicken mixture onto bottom of each bun; cover with bun tops.

VEGETABLE STEW

Kathy White
1 1/2 T. olive oil
1 medium onion, diced
2 carrots, peeled and large diced
2 stalks celery, large diced
2 T. flour
1 turnip, peeled and diced
2 parsnips, peeled and diced
1/2 mushrooms, quartered
1/2 tsp. garlic
1 c. tomatoes, diced
1 medium potato, diced
2 T. parsley, chopped
4 c. chicken or vegetable broth
1 1/2 c. water

Heat the oil in a soup pot. Add the onion, carrots and celery. Cook until just soft. Add the flour and cook for 3 minutes. Add the remaining ingredients; bring to a boil. Reduce heat and simmer.

EASY BRUNSWICK STEW

Kathy White
1 (4 to 5 lbs.) Boston butt pork roast
4 c. cubed hash brown potatoes
3 (14.5 oz) cans diced tomatoes with garlic and onion
1 (14.5 oz) can whole kernel corn, drained
1 (14.5 oz) can cream-style corn
1 (15.25 oz) can sweet green peas, drained
1 (16 oz) bottle barbecue sauce
1 T. hot sauce
1 tsp. salt
1 tsp. pepper

Cook pork roast in boiling water to cover in a stockpot 2 1/2 hours or until tender; drain, reserving 4 cups liquid. Cool roast lightly; shred meat with fork. Return reserved liquid to stockpot. Add hash brown potatoes and bring to a boil. Reduce heat and simmer 15 minutes. Add shredded pork, tomatoes, and remaining ingredients. Bring mixture to a boil; cover, reduce heat and simmer 1 hour. Yield: 5 quarts.

LOW COUNTRY BOIL

Kathy White

Fill Large pot (20 to 30 gallon) 1/2 full of water.

Add:

1/2 box salt
1/2 bottle garlic salt
1 small jar whole bay leaves
1/2 box Konrico Creole seasoning (hot and spicy)
2 pkg. crab boil (Zatarain's)

Bring to a rolling boil. **Add 5-7 pounds red potatoes (egg size, whole, unpeeled).** Cook for 20 minutes.

Add:

5 lb small whole onions
20-25 pieces corn on the cob
1 1/2 large bag peeled baby carrots
2 medium rutabaga, peeled and cubed 1 inch

Cook for 10 minutes.

Add:

5 lb. smoked sausage, cut in bite size
3 medium unpeeled sweet potatoes, cut in 3 inch pieces

Cook 10 minutes

Add:

3 heads cabbage, quartered
10lb headless unpeeled shrimp
5 oz lemon juice
5 oz vinegar

Stir good. Cut off heat; cover and let stand for 10 minutes. Will feed 25 people or 10 Tanners. Some like it better to omit the shrimp and double the sausage.

VEGETABLE RELISH

Wende Sumner
I c. onion, diced
I c. bell pepper, diced
I jar pimentos
I can Laseur English peas
I can white shoe peg corn
I c. sugar substitute
I c. apple cider vinegar

Melt and reduce sugar in vinegar over low heat in medium saucepan. Put all other ingredients in medium bowl. Mix well. Pour sugar mixture over top of vegetables and mix well. Refrigerate overnight.

HAM AND CHEESE QUICHE

Kathy White
1/2 c. diced cooked ham
5 beaten eggs
I ¼ c. half and half
1/2 c. shredded Swiss cheese
I c. shredded sharp cheddar cheese
2 T. all purpose flour
2 T. honey mustard
1/4 c. chopped green onions
1/4 tsp. salt
Pastry for 9 inch quiche

Line a 9 inch quiche dish with pastry; trim excess pastry around edges. Prick bottom and sides of pastry with fork. Bake at 400 degrees for 5 minutes.; remove from oven and gently prick with fork. Bake and additional 5 minutes. Combine Swiss cheese; 1/2 cup cheddar cheese; and I T. flour; toss gently. Sprinkle evenly in pastry shell. Combine ham and honey mustard, toss gently to coat. Spoon ham mixture over cheese. Combine eggs; half and half; green onion; remaining I T. flour and salt; stir well. Pour mixture into pastry shell; top with remaining ½ cup cheddar cheese. Bake at 350 degrees for 40 to 50 minutes or until set. Let stand 10 minutes before serving.

SLOW COOKER BRUNSWICK STEW
Wende Sumner
2 lbs boneless porkloin, cooked
4-6 boneless, skinless chicken breast, cooked
Put meats in food processor and process them until well shredded. Set aside.
1 frozen tube creamed corn
1 lrg can crushed tomatoes
1 (16 oz) pkg chicken broth
1/4 c. Worcestershire sauce
1/2 c. vinegar based barbecue sauce
1/2 c. sweet based barbecue sauce
1 medium onion, finely chopped
1/2 stick butter
1/2 tsp salt and pepper or more to taste
1/2 T. Old Bay seasoning

Sauté onion in butter until clear. Add all ingredients, including meats, into slow cooker and cook on low for 8-10 hours. Add more chicken broth or water as needed or as desired.

HOBO DINNER
Kathy White
Chicken
Onions
Bell Pepper
Desired Vegetables
Potatoes

On a piece of heavy duty aluminum foil, place seasoned chicken, potatoes, and veggies (I use carrots and broccoli). Sprinkle seasoning salt on veggies. Place onions and bell peppers on top of ingredients. Seal the foil and place on cookie sheet. Bake for one hour at 375 degrees. Note: Other meats can be used.

BLUEBERRY SALAD

Kathy White
2 (3 oz) boxes grape jello
1 (16 oz) can crushed pineapple (do not drain)
2 cups boiling water
1 can blueberry pie filling
1 c. chopped pecans
Topping:
1 (8 oz) cream cheese
1 (8 oz) carton sour cream
1/2 c. sugar
1 tsp. vanilla

Combine Jell-o and water and stir until dissolved. Add un-drained pineapple, nuts, pie filling and stir. Refrigerate until congealed.
Topping: Soften cream cheese. Combine all ingredients and whip until smooth. Spoon over top of congealed mixture.

EGG CUSTARD

Kathy White
6 eggs, well beaten
1 1/2 c. sugar substitute
1 can evaporated milk
1 can water
4 T. butter
1 T. vanilla (or nutmeg)
2 unbaked pie shells

Mix all ingredients (excluding pie shells, of course) and beat well. Cook at 375 degrees until brown (solid). Do not overcook.

HIGH PROTEIN BANANA BREAD
Kathy White
1/2 c. shortening
1 c. sugar substitute
2 eggs
3 large bananas, mashed
2 1/2 c. flour
8 T. milk
1 tsp. poppy seeds
1 tsp. baking soda
1 tsp. baking powder
pinch of salt
1 scoop unflavored protein powder

Cream together shortening, sugar, eggs, and bananas. Add balance of ingredients. Pour into greased and floured loaf pan and bake at 350 degrees for 35 minutes or until center tests done.

RICE PUDDING
Kathy White
1 1/3 T. margarine
1 1/2 c. hot, cooked rice
2 eggs
1 1/2 c. whole milk
7 T. sugar substitute
1 tsp. vanilla
dash of salt
dash of nutmeg
3/4 c. raisins (optional)
1 scoop protein powder (optional)

Stir margarine into rice. Beat eggs, add milk, sugar, vanilla, salt, nutmeg, raisins and protein powder. Stir rice into mixture. Pour into baking dish. Place in pan of hot water. Bake at 325 degrees for 30 minutes or until knife comes out clean. Stir gently several times during the first 20 minutes. Sprinkle with nutmeg.

PUMPKIN PIE
Kathy White
3 cups canned pumpkin
3 cups milk
3/4 c. sugar substitute
1/2 tsp. ginger
1/2 tsp. salt
1/2 tsp. allspice
1 tsp. cinnamon
3 T. flour
3 eggs
1 ready made pie crust

Combine all ingredients and mix well. Place mixture in a 9 inch ready made pie crust. Bake at 350 degrees for 45 minutes to 1 hour.

HIGH PROTEIN PEANUT BUTTER COOKIES
Kathy White
1 c. shortening
1 c. white sugar substitute
1 c. peanut butter
3 eggs
1 scoop unflavored protein
1 c. brown sugar substitute
1 tsp. baking soda
1 tsp. salt
2 3/4 c. flour

Mix shortening, sugar, peanut butter and eggs. Add brown sugar, protein, baking soda, salt and flour. Roll into balls. Bake at 400 degrees for 10 minutes.

INDEX
APPETIZERS & BEVERAGES

SOUPS & SALADS

Mushy Phase

VEGETABLES & SIDE DISHES

MAIN DISHES

BREADS & ROLLS

DESSERTS

ABOUT THE AUTHOR

Amy Solen is a happily married mother of three children. She currently lives in Georgia on a small farm where she raises goats, rabbits, chickens, turkeys and guineas. She has originally had Lap-Band® surgery in 2008 and had a revision to the biliopancreatic diversion with a duodenal switch in May of 2010. She has since lost over 145lbs from her highest weight and is happier than ever with her success thus far. She continues her journey on a daily basis and is always looking for new ways to help others who are embarking on their journeys. She can be found on Facebook at www.facebook.com/CookingafterWLS .

25087664R00084

Made in the USA
San Bernardino, CA
17 October 2015